Dirty Laundry

Dirty Laundry

Coloreds and Whites

Lavelle

iUniverse, Inc.
Bloomington

Dirty Laundry
Coloreds and Whites

iUniverse books may be ordered through booksellers or by contacting:

iUniverse
1663 Liberty Drive
Bloomington, IN 47403
www.iuniverse.com
1-800-Authors (1-800-288-4677)

ISBN: 978-1-4759-4890-5 (sc)
ISBN: 978-1-4759-4891-2 (hc)
ISBN: 978-1-4759-4892-9 (ebk)

Library of Congress Control Number: 2012916758

Printed in the United States of America

iUniverse rev. date: 09/21/2012

CONTENTS

Acknowledgments

I thank all those who have been an inspiration to me. First I give thanks to God, for without him nothing is possible. He gives us life and a chance to be whatever we want to be.

Thanks to my family, who have put up with me and been patient and understanding while I focused on writing this book. The bonds that I share with you give me the strength to go on when I feel like giving up. I thank all of my family and friends who have contributed to my growth and progress.

INTRODUCTION

I was born in the city of Chicago in 1971 and raised on the West Side. My family—my mother, father, and younger sister—lived in a six-unit apartment building, whose tenants included my grandmother, aunt and uncle, and several cousins. When I was around eight years old, my parents purchased a two-flat unit in an area called K-Town.

Growing up, I was lucky to have two parents who were concerned about how my life would turn out. I was cared for, nurtured, educated, and disciplined by both of them. They always taught me to think for myself and never be a follower. That philosophy became an almost unconscious, lifelong commitment and remains with me to this day.

Other family members provided the same sort of love, caring, and discipline. It is how most of my relatives escaped some of hardships that befall many families. My siblings, cousins, and friends had options that were provided by our surroundings, family members, and friends; as a result, we had more opportunities to choose what our lives would be like. Whether we always made good decisions is another matter, but the choices were there.

By 1980, we also had politicians in the family, so I had an early interest in city and state government. I regularly read the *Illinois*

Handbook of Government during my teenage years. I kept up with the races for alderman, mayor, governor, and Congress. At one time, knowing the players in my city and state was very important to me.

As a black man, obviously race relations are important to me as well. I don't feel that my race has held me back in any kind of way; I never use it as a crutch or an excuse for failure. But I also didn't grow up during the 1950s and 1960s or in the hundreds of years prior to that, when just being black could be considered a crime.

Since those days, blacks have made strides in the media, sports, and business as well. Despite these successes, something doesn't seem right. We can all see it, although some choose to ignore it. The issue cannot be ignored any longer; something has got to be done. Some things need to be cleaned up. So today is laundry day.

CHAPTER 1

CHANGE

One definition of *change* is the transformation from one state, condition, or phase to another. The word *change* was heard a lot during the 2008 presidential campaign. It became an effective rallying cry for getting Barack Obama elected president of the United States.

Now that we are done with the "yes, we can" slogans, let's look some of what's changed. Unemployment is high, between 8 percent and 10 percent; banks that received bailouts are not sharing the wealth; and homes are being foreclosed, leaving many homeless. Poverty is greater than I can ever recall. Americans are unhappy and suffering, and the blame is being placed on the two entities that are almost always in bed with each another: the government and big business. The Occupy demonstrations that took place in major cities like New York, Chicago, and Oakland in 2011 and 2012 are evidence that many people are angry and don't like the current state of the nation.

Those who protest social or political issues often are effective in bringing about change in this country and abroad. Labor laws and the civil rights and voting rights acts all started with someone or

1

a group of people who were unhappy with the status quo. Once again, the country is demanding change.

It's nice to see members of organizations like the Tea Party voicing their opinions and winning seats nationwide. It is about time that someone stepped up and questioned the leaders of this country about the decisions being made on Capitol Hill, which some say are destroying the fabric of America. Even if, as Politics USA wrote that Tea Party members are on the same wavelength as the Ku Klux Klan (KKK) as far as their ideology and bigoted philosophy with notions of protecting liberty and returning to the strictest interpretation of the Constitution. KKK aside, in talking to others as well as my following the news and current events, the point is; that people are questioning and challenging the direction and leadership of this country, and that is a good thing.

And it is not only the Tea Party. Many people—black, Latino, and white—are complaining about the choices made by elected leaders. Some, like me, would like to tear down most of the current political structure, starting by getting rid of the gatekeeping black officials who go along with the ideology of rich, sometimes racist whites, while paying lip service to the pitiful blacks who believe that those in power hold the key to their happiness. The United States of America has a history of oppressing and excluding people, from American Indians to Africans. How can one avoid becoming an oppressor himself after joining such an entity?

This is why I have such a hard time trusting most elected officials, including those who are black. That should not be surprising. I am a black man in America; as some see it that is my crime. For that reason alone, I see the government as an entity that will harass, abuse, and lock black people up for life or carry out the death penalty on them.

My black elected officials, where are the laws that stop racial profiling? Why are there disparities in jail time for using or dealing crack cocaine and powder cocaine? What about enacting laws that prosecute and punish racist white cops who kill unarmed blacks? Instead they get gold medals for lying their tails off after they kill somebody's son or daughter. Have you passed any laws that make it harder for a black man to be jailed or put to death for a crime that he did not commit? What about laws that prosecute companies that deny jobs to people simply because they made mistakes in their youth and went to prison, even though they've paid their debts to society?

Things have gotten worse for a lot of people in this country. In the wake of the housing crisis and 2008 market crash, many people have lost their jobs and their homes. Middle-class Americans of all races are struggling, which is why this crisis is real and not simply an instance of poor, black people complaining while they sit on their butts doing nothing.

If white America is suffering from a cold in the aftermath of the 2008 economic crisis, then black America must be suffering from the flu. If hardworking, non-black Americans are feeling the crunch—losing their jobs and homes—where do the poor, black people stand in all this?

Unfortunately, black people as a group are divided and, as such, they are in a house that cannot stand. It probably can't get much worse from a unity standpoint; black-on-black crime and ignorance are running black people into the ground. Things can get better, though. If people would only focus on their commonalities, the black race could achieve a more prominent place in society. It's hard to challenge the direction of the country when many of your people lag behind everyone else in wealth, education, and social position.

Currently, quite a few black people hold government office, probably more now than at any other time in the history of the United States. Some continue to be elected despite the fact that the districts or wards they represent have constituents who are at the bottom of the social ladder, although many of their non-black counterparts don't even speak the English language.

In my opinion, many black people in government have joined the club. They seek power and prestige, supporting their counterparts by raising taxes, depleting Social Security, and allowing big business and special-interest groups to have their way. Meanwhile, the American people suffer.

The gap between the rich and the poor is increasing, and in many black communities across America—given the poverty, crime, filth, and ignorance that exist there—the conditions are like the Third World. Why do we continue to elect officials who have outgrown their usefulness, when desperation and despair engulfs so many?

Black America, I vote that, for now, we put all current politics and politicians on hold. Only with an establishment of a new party, with new people and new ideas, should black people come to the table and begin again. I'm not trying to stop you from voting; I'm just saying that it's time to wake up and smell the coffee. You should value your vote, not give it to a particular party or individual simply because that's the way it is.

We need more black doctors, teachers, lawyers, business owners, dentists, and construction companies. These are the individuals who can make a difference in the lives of black youth and serve as inspirations to the generations that follow. It's time to build, people.

The way to ensure that black America is more united and has solid economic and social standing is right in front of our face and has nothing to do with politics. Unfortunately, many either refuse to act, are part of the problem, or simply don't care. Others would rather beg or blame others, or believe that President Obama will wave a magic wand and uplift the black race after a count of three.

People elect these officials and then act surprised that things in their part of the world are the same or worse. Nothing will change until we build a better foundation, neighborhood by neighborhood, city by city, and state by state. If the politicians do decide to help or get involved with this process, good, the more the merrier, as long as their intentions are sincere and not simply for votes or publicity. But believing that someone else is responsible for your wellbeing or to ensure you have a better life is childish. Thoughts like that have to go in the big pot, along with the other inhibitors that keep black people at the bottom of the social ladder.

It's way past time to uplift the black race to a better place in society. The community as a whole has major problems. There are not enough black businesses in predominately black areas; fewer black males are going to college or even finishing high school. If things continue in this way, there will be a high number of uneducated and ignorant brothers and sisters in the future, surrounded by a higher number of striving or successful people from other races. Such a situation could send black people back to the cotton fields. Without a legitimate income, education, and respect for oneself and others, what else will black youth face in the future, if not slavery?

The time has run out for politics, or at least politics in its current state. I include groups like the National Association for the Advancement of Colored People (NAACP), Rainbow/PUSH, and other so-called black-focused groups in this assessment. Despite the existence of numerous black organizations, the state of black America seems to have regressed. What is the real purpose of such groups?

I have never trusted these organizations because I believe they have their own agendas, are puppets on a string that are controlled by white people, and seek funds from the government solely so they can become wealthy. In my opinion, they are also an ineffective driving force within black America. Those organizations, like every able black man, woman, boy, or girl in this country, need to be held accountable for their actions. In essence, they need to take up a broom or a shovel, shine some shoes, and get to work.

Black America is either in or heading toward a crisis, depending on your point of view. Instead of being brainwashed by groups or individuals and focusing on being accepted by other races, we need to take up the reins, pull up our bootstraps, and build, build, build. Let our work speak for itself and earn the respect that we seek.

Anyone who is poor and lives in an impoverished community needs to know that there isn't a politician on this earth who can make your neighborhood prosperous or crime free. Communities need industry and businesses run by those who live there, not talk and speeches.

If your councilman or representative doesn't own a business, how can he give you a job? How can he clean up your neighborhood? He can create the climate for business to excel, but without the businesses and services that a prosperous community has, things will never change.

Are elected officials supposed to give a job to every unemployed person in a district, ward, city, or state? It's amazing how many people believe that someone other than themselves and God can improve their lives.

Many need to stop thinking that the government or organizations is the cure to all that ails us. God helps those that help themselves, as the saying goes. If you want something, you go after it and work for it. And you will get it. Construction, engineering, and architecture are examples of careers that have great earning potential. These are some of the fields in which young black people are needed and can make a good living.

While everyone won't be wealthy, you can live somewhat comfortably if you choose to do so. It depends on how hard you work and how smart you are with your money. One way to feel like you are a part of a process or part of a community is by doing your part. It starts with making a living if you are healthy and taking care of yourself and your family, if you have one.

You want representation? You need blocks of home ownership, respectful neighbors, and children attending school. You need neighbors who are working and own businesses. You need medical and dental services.

My community has very few black-owned neighborhood restaurants and corner stores. The mom-and-pop stores that once existed are now owned by immigrants, who serve chicken, steak sandwiches, and pizza puffs to the black community. This is not a knock on other ethnic groups; they're running their businesses and trying to make a living, as everyone has a right to do. Rather, this is a knock on the black race.

If we took a poll right now, asking members of all races across this nation which race lacks the most, which one would be said to have the most despair? Which would be number two? What would the survey tell us? The results might terrify some individuals but be of no surprise to others, I bet.

As long as the black base is nonexistent, things will remain exactly the same or get worse. Since the black base is weak, there is no real representation, only promises that are never kept. In many cases, there is nothing to represent. But if the work is done to build a better base for black America, there will be no need to look to politicians or others for help. Instead, they will look to us to see if we need help with anything. The more prosperous and prominent that black America becomes, the better off the United States will be. Until that happens, most will continue to hear plenty of talk, with little or no action.

You might ask, "What do you mean? President Obama is going to change everything, remember?" That is what the naïve and misguided were saying in 2008.

Those who want to relish the moment he was elected president should feel free to do so. I always feel the same, regardless of who is sitting in the White House. My entertainment level varies from president to president, depending on who is in office at the time. Many black people disliked George W. Bush, but I thought he was funny and enjoyed hearing him speak.

Since Ronald Reagan's presidency, I have tried to stay current on governmental affairs. I remember when Reagan was elected, but I was only nine years old in 1980, too young to understand what was going on. As I grew older though, I began to pay attention to the president, vice president, speaker of the House of Representatives, senators, and congressmen. Of course, race was not a factor in most elections for president, governor, or senator. In most presidential elections, the only choices have been to vote white or not to vote at all. Before Obama, only six black candidates ran for president: Frederick Douglas in 1888; Shirley Chisholm in 1972; Jesse Jackson in 1984 and 1988; Alan Keyes in 1992, 1996, 2000, and 2008; and Carol Moseley Braun and Al Sharpton in 2004.

I did not vote for Obama simply because he was black. In fact, I didn't vote for him at all. I didn't have the sense that there was history was being made. My thoughts were, *They put this guy in the front, surrounded by whites, with no ties to anything black or the struggle to be black in America. And because he looks somewhat like me I'm supposed to think that black people in America have arrived?* Even so, I congratulate him for being elected and I am pleased that we have a black first lady, who was raised by two black parents in the city of Chicago. This is a first in American history and a moment that should be relished.

There were some people who didn't vote for Obama *because* he was black, a low blow even by this country's standards. Considering that the previous forty-three presidents have all been white, one would think that even the most racist hate mongers would conclude that one out of forty-four isn't such bad odds. Looking at it any other way is just *stupid*. Of course, I know that all presidents endure criticism from one group or another. But let's be honest, some of the criticism of Barack Obama is because he is black.

Regardless, he has filled his cabinet with more white people than black, just like every other president. So let's wait and see if he accomplishes anything before we start celebrating. If he started a movement that brought an end to the hate and violence perpetrated by many young black people, then that would be history. If state supreme courts or the US Supreme Court had half as many black judges as they do white ones, that too would be history.

A black president is in the White House, and all hell breaks loose. Now, a bad economy, the unstable stock market, healthcare debates, and the high rate of unemployment are recurring topics in this country. A lot of the blame for these things is placed at Obama's feet. This is what I and others were wary about when Obama was elected. We believed that if America elected a black president, it meant the shit was about to hit the fan, and the establishment would blame it on him.

Some compared Obama as Martin Luther King Jr. Some tried to connect the famous "I have a dream" speech to Obama's speech when he accepted the Democratic nomination for president. Obama referred to King as "a preacher from Atlanta" rather than as "Dr. Martin Luther King Jr." But some naive people try to draw some comparison between the two by comparing photos of both King and Obama in deep thought and passing them around. Maybe Obama was being poetic when he called King a preacher from Atlanta instead of by his name in both his Democratic nomination and President elect acceptance speech. In some of my close circles of friends we discussed if maybe Dr. King was not recognized by name intentionally, as a way to not offend white America, and more importantly, as a way to win white votes.

King dealt with race-related issues. Obama has not. King marched and was beaten and arrested; he was spied on and betrayed by black FBI agents who infiltrated his organization under the order of white officials. The only thing Obama and King have in common is their skin color, period. After all the years of struggle, despite efforts by Abraham Lincoln, Dwight Eisenhower, John F Kennedy and Lyndon Johnson, to deal with issues of race, President Obama makes statements like he is the President of all people in America and not just black people. But during Obama's presidency the ban on gays in the military has been lifted, gay marriage is allowed in some states and there has been immigration reform for Latinos. Does this means that gays and Latino rights are the focus and take more precedence than black issues?

Some will say that, "President Obama can't have a black agenda because of what white America will think." If black people in America have arrived, however, then now is the time for a black agenda. What better time than with a black president at the helm? Of course, the other possibility is that black people haven't really arrived and have much more work to do. Or maybe Obama isn't the first black president.

I know that some blacks believe that it doesn't matter whether Obama turns out to be a good or bad president. The fact that most believe he is the first black president gives him a free pass. Why? Because in their minds, black people have been screwed by so many white presidents in the past, why not give a brother a chance? After all, "if he does screw me, at least I will have been screwed by someone who looks like me." It is the equivalent of an individual rubbing your stomach with one hand while using the other hand to reach into your pocket and take your money.

The phrase "painting the White House black" is used in some circles. Some have joked about barbecues and stepping taking place on the White House lawn. I don't think we have to worry. The White House remains what it always has been, which is *white*, of course. No matter whom the president is or who sits in Congress, we seem to get more of the same. The country is still serving as Big Brother abroad, helping other countries to establish democracies while slowly limiting our own democracy and freedom. Other countries receive aid, while many here in the United States continue to starve. Many of our roads and bridges have potholes and are worn and need repairing. Jobs that were once available in this country have been taken overseas, away from Americans citizens, as a way of getting cheap labor.

To be honest, there are those who don't care about having a job, the conditions of the roads, or about anything. But there are millions of unhappy Americans who have a right to complain about the current conditions and direction of this country. If it isn't right, it isn't right, and you can count me among those who are dissatisfied with the state of America today.

Let me clear up a big misconception. Many young people say they want to work, but will only work high-paying jobs. They view working at fast-food restaurants or cleaning up bathrooms as demeaning and insulting. I too hated cleaning up the eating area and the bathroom when I worked at McDonald's. But I did what I had to do to earn my own money when I was sixteen and seventeen years old. I took great pride in being able to buy some of my own school clothes or to have money for food and movies.

Today, jobs are hard to come by. But prior to the 2008 recession, one could find work if one wanted to. It may or may not have been the ideal job, but you could still find some kind of job. What many people don't seem to get is that you have to start somewhere. Eventually, you may find a better job or you may move up in your position and/or pay. I once worked for a company that didn't pay much, a truck-driving job. I found a higher-paying job after I met a gentleman on my route who told me about openings at his company. Once I finished my route, I drove the truck to the other company, and I got the job. At the time, it was the highest salary that I had ever been paid.

If you are broke, complaining won't get you anywhere. Holding up signs that state "We want jobs" may get you publicity but it will not necessarily get you work. Some simply do this to be involved in something; they go along with the crowd because they have nothing else to do that day. But who respects a beggar? You have to take what you want, I don't mean by robbing and hurting other individuals. Make your way through life, and get what you want through hard work.

There is too much false pride among those aged sixteen to twenty-four. To hear some speak about what amount of money and what job they will or won't do is interesting, to say the least. One of the more classic lines I've heard is "I have no skill or training, but I refuse to work at a particular place because the pay is so cheap. I need $12 or $14 an hour." Some would rather be broke and depend on others than work at Burger King for "little money." I've also heard a young girl bragging that she and her brother were not going to school, and it was only the second week of classes. It's amazing what you hear. Far too many black people sit on their rear ends and refuse to go to school, learn a trade, or do anything.

The jobs are available, but the ambition is not. The real truth or real problem is that many don't want to work, period. Some would rather do anything else; others destroy the community by being the main physical threat against black people in this country.

If black people, especially the young, don't get their act together, there will be no future for us at all. With the continuing trend of black-on-black crime, drug abuse, the high incarceration rate, and ignorance, how can the black race move forward with confidence? How can it move at all?

Black people don't need politicians or speeches. They need to pull themselves up by their bootstraps, stop complaining, and stop blaming. Black America needs a rebirth, a start over. The time for talk is over; it's time for action.

Many black officials give us a lot of talk so we will elect them. They promise change, and talk about some of the problems that plague us, that black people themselves are mostly to blame. You mostly hear this rhetoric during an election. After they are elected, however, most officials continue the business-as-usual attitude, the status quo, which prevails in federal, state, and local government.

Many of these officials are gatekeepers, in my opinion. They stand in the way and prevent black people from seeing the real solutions to the problems that exist today. In effect, they keep most things the way they are for the weak and desperate, who continue to believe in them.

Turn off the television. Get off of Facebook and Twitter, and put the cell phones down. It's time to get down to business. It's been more than forty years, black people. Dr. King isn't coming back to take us to the Promised Land. What have black people done for themselves lately? Why not come up with something new? When are black people going to move on?

CHAPTER 2

CHICAGO-STYLE POLITICS

Chicago, Second City, the Windy City, Chi Town, or whatever you want to call it, has always had a unique style of politics, dominated by the Democratic and very powerful machine created by Anton Cermak, mayor from 1931 to 1933. It was perfected by later mayors Pat Nash, Ed Kelly, and the infamous Richard J. Daley, among others.

So far, the machine has produced five mayors, all from the Bridgeport area on the southwest side. Kelly was the first. Bridgeport was like many communities in the United States. If you were black and caught there after dark (or even in the day), you'd get your ass kicked or be killed by intolerant whites.

For example, in 2010 comedian George Wilborn attempted to purchase a home in Bridgeport for 1.7 million dollars. He was denied by the homeowners and the real estate agent and inevitably, along with the Urban Housing development suing both the homeowner, the real estate agent and his firm; Prudential Rubloff Properties. For decades, places like Bridgeport, Cicero, or Marquette Park didn't allow my kind to live or even visit without being confronted with hatred and violence. So I wouldn't ever, ever want to live in those areas even if I live to be one hundred years old. I was chased out of Cicero by white boys in my youth, and I've heard numerous stories of blacks being harassed and assaulted in Bridgeport. I wouldn't dream of putting my family at risk just to prove a point. Chicago has a history of oppression, exclusion, and segregation. As a resident of the city, and based on what I have read and been told by others older than myself, I can say this is an accepted way of life.

Most black people who want to succeed politically in the city have to be approved by or join the machine to do so. An independent can have a successful run, but he will face constant challenges, usually from another black person who is controlled by the Democratic Party. And since many blacks don't have the guts or the brains to switch to the Republican Party or form a new one, this trend will probably continue in Chicago for the foreseeable future.

In 1983, Chicago elected its first and so far only black mayor. Harold Washington was anti-machine and even formed his own party, the Harold Washington Party. Washington was able to unite blacks, Latinos, and some whites who felt change was needed. They were tired of Chicago politics and its history of racism and exclusion. Washington was reelected in 1987 but died early in his second term.

Two aldermen on the city council and their allies challenged Washington: Ed Burke, a former cop, and Edward Vrdolyak, known as Fast Eddie. Vrdolyak has a colorful personality. Despite his fights with Mayor Washington, I can tolerate him. However, in my opinion, Burke is a control freak, a denier of rights, and a suppressor of freedom. I can only imagine what type of policeman he was.

These two men formed what became known as the Vrdolyak 29, a group of twenty-nine white councilmen who opposed the mayor's initiatives. The other twenty-one aldermen who sided with the mayor could not override the votes of the twenty-nine. That made it difficult for the mayor to carry through any of his initiatives. The dispute was known as the Council Wars, and many of the meetings were full of emotion and tension between Washington and his foes.

During one interview during the news I marveled in hearing Mayor Washington speak of how every morning before he went to work he would look in the mirror and ask, "I wonder what old Fast Eddie and Burke have planned for me today." He truly was remarkable during the Council Wars and handled himself superbly from what I saw on the news or heard from family members who were involved with politics. Articulate and fiery, he was the first black man who could handle the pressure of being mayor despite the racist whites and gatekeeping blacks on the council and in the city.

Harold Washington was not a figurehead who met the black quota; he was really a good politician who knew how things worked. When he died in 1987, the Harold Washington Party and the always fragile black unity in Chicago died with him. Had he not died in office, I believe that things would have been much different in Chicago, assuming other black officials did not sell him out.

Judge and former Alderman Timothy Evans, Judge Eugene Pincham and former Alderman Dorothy Tillman (who, by the way, had more guts than most of the black men on the city council), and a few others tried to keep the Washington Party afloat. But as usual, the machine-backed black candidates, power-hungry black pastors, and those eager to be called the machine's "favorite Negro" made sure that this was not to be. Since 1987, no black person has been elected mayor of Chicago, although black people are still the majority population (even if slightly) in the city.

The greed and delusions of grandeur that I see often seems to get in the way of what's best for the black masses and the ways to continue growth as a whole, and not just personally. Why is it so hard for black people in Chicago to agree on and get behind one candidate? Damn, three or five people can't win one seat. Why not get together and agree to support one candidate, and let the others hold positions in the new administration? Can you defer your ambitions to be king or queen for four years? It's an embarrassing charade, and it is shameful enough for me to accept that black unity is finished in Chicago.

When Mayor Richard M. Daley, the son of previous mayor Richard J. Daley, who I mentioned above, announced after more than twenty years in office that he would not seek reelection in 2011, it sent shock waves through the city. What happened after that was both historic and also the saddest display of politics I've ever seen. There was a useless forum held to pick a consensus black candidate. It was useless because after all the talk, there was no agreement. Instead, there were seven goofballs, each saying that he was the consensus pick for the mayor's seat.

Despite the financial gains realized by some Chicago politicians, black people are still crabs at the bottom of the barrel—unless you consider being loyal to the machine and being able to give jobs to family and friends equal to having real power. If that's enough to satisfy the black masses in Chicago, so be it. Many of the black politicians in Chicago seem to have inflated egos and dream of being the boss so much that they don't realize the opposite is true: they're actually cronies and gatekeepers.

I have to ask the three black candidates who campaigned for mayor in 2011—Carol Moseley Braun, Dock Walls, and Patricia Watkins: *How in the world were all three of you going to win the black vote?* Just as disturbing, *Why didn't your campaign managers and staffers, family, and friends ask you the same question?* If you can't win the black vote in Chicago, you can't win a major election, such as for county board president or mayor. A big part of the dominance of the Chicago Democratic machine comes from receiving the majority of the black vote during mayoral and other citywide elections.

For black candidates, however, the need to win the black vote is twice as important. If you can't get the majority of your own people to support you, how will you cross racial lines in significant numbers? How will you win a citywide or statewide election? If two or more black candidates run in the same race, it will be impossible for either one to win the black vote. In the end, Moseley Braun, Walls, and Watkins were defeated, just as I expected, and Rahm Emmanuel was elected mayor in a landslide, winning 59 percent of the Black vote along the way. He became the first Jewish mayor of Chicago.

During the Richard M. Daley years, any black opposition was crushed at election time. Occasionally, Daley won more black votes in a candidate's own area than the candidate did himself. With the help of the black church and elected officials, and other ring kissers, so to speak, he was able to prevent a strong candidate from ever rising from within the black community. If black candidates were too weak or afraid to challenge Daley during his twenty-two-year reign, why did they run in 2011? Did some people get stronger despite all the years of bowing down? Maybe their egos have grown, but how strong can you be after twenty-two years of kissing Daley's ring. I didn't hear much of a real plan from any of the black candidates; some of them had been in politics for years but didn't accomplish much. And now they want to be the mayor of Chicago? I don't think so.

Many voters saw what I saw: three losers making a mockery of the election process. They decided to vote for the person best able to move the city forward. The only thing is, this is Chicago, and if it was "all hail the king" during the Daley years, I don't know if there is a crown big enough for Emmanuel's head. The reins are going to be pulled even tighter, and a lot of people are going to be taxed on everything from candy and bottled water, to gas and cigarettes.

During the city's first mayoral election in more than sixty years without an incumbent running, I witnessed many things. I witnessed the fear that Emmanuel's candidacy put into the hearts of many. I saw candidates worried about whether Emmanuel had legal residency, since he'd leased his home when he became President Obama's chief of staff. There were so many insecurities and so much focus on the sideshow, rather than on the issues, I knew one thing for sure: it would be a two-man race between Emmanuel and Daley's chief of staff, Gerry Chico. The black candidates' agendas and campaigns were so weak, in my opinion, that even if Emmanuel hadn't decided to run, there was no chance Chicago would have elected its second black mayor.

There is little in the history of Chicago politics that suggest otherwise. Only two individuals, Harold Washington, and Jane Byrne, the first woman elected as mayor in Chicago, have been able to successfully challenge the machine. If black people are to survive politically in Chicago or anywhere, they must change the way they view politics. It isn't a business that manufactures goods. It is not an opportunity to move to a higher tax bracket without having to work hard.

The public doesn't owe politicians anything because they've been elected. What have they done? Do they have careers? Do they own businesses or properties? Don't get me wrong, having a career prior to politics or being successful doesn't guarantee that you'd make a good politician. But isn't it obvious that twenty candidates are running for the same alderman's seat because it pays more than $100,000 a year? In my opinion, if the alderman's salary was $40,000, you'd never see twenty black candidates running for the seat.

Without their political careers or large bank accounts to back them up, some public officials would be no better off financially or socially than the average citizen. What I see in black politics is many who are simply trying to make a dollar, and some who

19

are willing to lie, cheat, be flunkies for the Democratic party, or steal to reach and maintain that status. When you show me an individual who has not made much money and does not have income equal to or greater than the salary of seat that he is running for, I see someone who can be corrupted, who is looking for an easy payday, power, and prestige.

Most, though not all, get into office and do what others do: maintain the status quo. The wealthy and the special-interest groups are usually the ones who are protected and whose interests are protected by many elected officials. Meanwhile, people see increases in taxes and fees and decreases in rights and freedoms. In Chicago, black pastors, community activists, and politicians all help to preserve the power of Irish families like the Daley's, Madigan's, and Burkes. Politically, as they say, they have Chicago on "lock" meaning they have all the power, the rest are spokes in the wheel which is the Democratic machine of Chicago.

I know that the government of the United States is tilted to one side, favoring the wealthy and powerful. We the people elect wealthy and influential people who represent the wealthy and the powerful. There are also the cronies, who claim to represent us but in actuality represent no one but themselves. Some are more than willing to go along with the wealthy and powerful, no matter the outcome. The average yearly income for a congressman is almost $200,000 and some of the people they represent earn millions and billions every year.

It's the cronies who concern me. Whether I like it or not, I am used to worldwide domination by white people. I am an American after all, and for more than four hundred years the white majority has ruled politically and socially in this country. Some of this dominance has been aided by black people, and that's where I have a problem. It is as if there were black men wearing hoods in the KKK, getting ready to burn a cross on someone's lawn.

Many elected black officials in Chicago have become imitators of their white counterparts, copying how they conduct business. For example, former alderman Ike Caruthers went to jail after accepting more than $40,000 in home improvements from a land developer, who made millions thanks to a zoning change made by Caruthers. It was all over the news and in both the Chicago Sun times and Chicago Tribune. This imitation as well as the psychological deficiencies that have endured since slavery are two of the reasons black men and women are willing to be used during elections. In Illinois, in classic machine fashion, I believe that many have purposely run for office, not because they want the seat, but to split the black vote to ensure that another black individual won't win.

What's the point of electing a wannabe when we have the real thing? There is no need, in my view, for striving to become an elected official, since it is the "master's" show anyway. Let's remove the cronies and concentrate on what's important and what we can change—ourselves and our communities.

If the 1980s era in Chicago City Council politics was known as the Council Wars, the Richard M. Daley years should be called the Rubber Stamp Days. The aldermen went along with whatever the mayor said. At times, it seemed as if his was the only voice on the council that counted. With an occasional dissenter (and that may be stretching it), Daley had almost total control over most of the bills he wanted to enact. Many black council members were there for the $100,000 salary and didn't want to cause any problems or controversy. Instead, they sucked up to the mayor and the more powerful councilmen.

No one said a thing when Daley took over the reins of the board of education in 1995, thanks to the Illinois General Assembly giving him and the mayor's office more power and decreasing the leverage held by the teachers union. A bigger blow was dealt by Daley's successor Rahm Emmanuel, who seems to be on the attack of public teachers who continue to be the focus as many kids continue to under perform. It is not the teachers' fault that far too many bad and undisciplined kids have been given a pass despite their clear lack of interest in school.

Public Schools in Chicago are 80 percent black and Latino. Before the power grab by Daley in 1995 and the bullying by Mayor Rahm Emmanuel in 2012, the Chicago Board of Education reflected the black and Latino population. Now white officials, including the Mayor himself send their own children to private schools, not public schools and yet, want to decide the future of black and Latino children. What are the gate-keeping black officials in Illinois doing about this power move? Absolutely nothing, kissing the ring as they've always been.

Chicago has been ranked as one of the most restrictive and miserable cities in America in surveys that rank the best and miserable places to live according to a poll I saw. The weather is one reason; others include laws and ordinances that I believe are oppressive and dictatorial. Chicago is indeed a miserable city, as far as I'm concerned. I've thought about moving to California, but I am afraid of earthquakes; however, Michigan is starting to look more attractive.

Chicago has more red-light cameras than any other US city as reported on CNN. In effect, it is the Big Brother for traffic violations and invasions of privacy, operating under the pretense of watching out for criminals. Politicians speak about cutting costs and decreasing debt, but they could start by eliminating these eyesores or traffic cameras which make some neighborhoods look worse than they really are. Instead of hiring more cops to protect the citizens and making the police do their jobs, the city would rather spend the money on traffic cameras.

In 2010, the Supreme Court overturned Chicago's handgun ban and ruled it unconstitutional. The ban had been enacted in 1982, despite the fact that the Second Amendment gives citizens the right to bear arms. In typical Chicago fashion, they balked at the supreme courts decision and while allowing hand gun ownership, it requires background checks, a firearm safety course, fingerprinting and fees. The gun ban hurts only those who are law abiding and are looking not to harm anyone, but only to defend themselves and their families. Those who are looking to harm, rob, assault, and murder others don't care about handgun bans. Street criminals aren't taking firearm safety courses or paying fees, they're shooting people. In Chicago, only the police and the criminals are armed, while the rest of us, the honest, hardworking citizens, are the victims of the criminals, and if you're black, the criminals and the police.

Some black aldermen are such products of this environment; they themselves create the ordinances that take away rights. One example includes the banning of smoking in public places like restaurants, bars, and bus and train stations, which was supported by former alderman Ed Smith. Mr. Smith also told a black congregation that black people who didn't vote for Barack Obama in 2012 would lose their food stamps. Is that what blacks want from Obama—food stamps? No wonder black people remain at the bottom of the social ladder in the United States. The gatekeepers are holding them there. The oppressed have become the oppressors.

Why are 90 percent of those arrested for marijuana possession black, while only 2 percent are white? There is also the continuing trend of police harassment and brutality. You'd think a black official would be concerned with real issues, instead of imitating his white counterparts who desire to control the lives of others and decide what is best for everyone.

I favor cutting the number of aldermen from fifty down to twenty-five, which was mentioned by then-Mayor-elect Rahm Emmanuel. It would be great to get rid of all the phonies, cronies, and imitators. Then we would see who the real politicians were, and send the losers to make a living like the rest of us. The city council, as far as I'm concerned, is a joke and a waste of the taxpayer's money. We do not need fifty aldermen to represent the fifty wards when, for the most part, they almost always agree. Where is the democracy in that?

When Mayor Washington was in office, he was given hell on a daily basis simply because he was black and would not play by the machine's rules. However, for the most part, Mayor Daley got a pass and was even helped by black aldermen to maintain his power and the power of the white, Irish-controlled Democratic machine. Such behavior is simply incredible, but common in Chicago politics. The shadiness of government and the shady politicians contribute to why many young blacks neither vote nor care about the candidates. As far as many are concerned, it's the same old story no matter who is in office. And they're absolutely correct in that regard; they see what goes on.

Daley was a very charismatic mayor. He was outspoken and tough. I enjoyed listening to him speak during press conferences or during his dealings with the nosy media. I remember watching the evening news, at one meeting in Humboldt Park, gang members were present, and some of them began to boo him. In a classic Daley moment, he said something like "locking up the dope dealers and gangbangers" loud and clear, making sure that everyone in the room could hear.

Chicago under Daley underwent a type of facelift. Many restaurants, new homes, condos, lofts, and venues in the downtown area were built during his years in office. He did, in fact, keep the city moving forward. But he also allowed his associates to enrich themselves through no-bid contracts in areas like construction, sewage repair and maintenance, and trucking according to stories reported by a Chicago Sun Times investigation

According to the rules of the Hired truck program that started in 1996, 25 percent of the trucking contracts are supposed to be set aside for Blacks, Latinos and women. However, black companies get nowhere near their entitled percentage of the work; there always will be some white individuals within the city departments who deny black-owned companies a fair share. Other times unfortunately, blacks simply don't have the equipment or manpower needed to complete a project.

Some light was shed on the behavior and actions of some companies and individuals during the hired truck scandal that was made public by a Chicago Sun Times investigation in 2004. Companies were bribing city officials to ensure they received the best and most profitable contracts. Some companies were billing the city for work they had not performed, and some even stole tons and tons of dirt.

It was found out during the Sun Times investigation that the white, male owners of some companies were using white women and black males as fronts so they could obtain contracts set aside for minorities. One black owner would receive a contract then subcontract it to a white company, and the two would split the profit. When all was revealed, he was told that he would no longer receive city contracts. The wannabe was out, but the companies he subcontracted work to are still doing business with the city.

Despite this type of corruption, the show must go on, so the city resumes to raising taxes, installing more traffic cameras (to increase fines), and reducing the amount of parking tickets required to qualify cars for the boot. They targeted side streets in black neighborhoods for seatbelt violations and developed other petty tactics to generate revenue The funny or sad part is that now street walking traffic cops come to the poor areas of the city and target and ticket cars who have expired vehicle registration. They won't walk the beat to stop the crime and the murder in many neighborhoods, but will give you a ticket for an expired sticker.

The mayor was allowed to shortchange the city on a $1 billion, seventy-five-year parking meter deal that could have netted more and raises parking fees for the people on a yearly basis as well. Only after the deal was done did Daley realize that he could have gotten more to privatize the parking meters. The current setup is also an inconvenience for citizens. Parking-garage attendants have been replaced by machines. On the street, one parking meter in the middle of the block has to service several cars rather than the one-car, one-meter setup that we've been accustomed to.

Despite the crime and corruption in Chicago, the focus seems to be more on higher gas cost and taxes, on hurting the average citizen. The connected ones continue to have their way in the city, while others go along with the show, just as long as they get a crumb of the pie.

A lot of people I know, even my friends and family, were so sure that Chicago would get the 2016 Olympics. Many felt that it would be great for the city. A lot of people were excited about the possibility of Chicago hosting the games. Major construction would have taken place on the lakefront, Washington Park, and Douglas Park. I wanted to believe how great it would be for Chicago, but then I thought, *Yeah, it will be great for the ones who usually receive all the major construction projects.* The money and the exposure that the Olympics would have given Chicago would have been a great and a real benefit, but for whom? "They don't deserve it!" I shouted when it was announced that Chicago did not win the bid; it went to Rio de Janeiro. I loved every minute of it. It was nice to see the disappointment of the arrogant individuals who had been so sure. It was a small victory, but I thank God for justice!

The smoking ban on airplanes was initiated by a Chicago native, Senator Dick Durbin, the same man who lobbies for the banning of chewing tobacco in Major League Baseball.

CHAPTER 3

RACE IN THE WORLD

I am not a believer in using the race card anytime someone I know is not hired for a job or given a promotion. There are instances in which others are simply more qualified. But job discrimination has existed since jobs have been available in this country. The Statue of Liberty was a welcoming sign for foreign immigrants to the land of opportunity despite the hundreds of years of free labor and suffering by black Americans. It was clear which group would have to fight the hardest to survive.

That doesn't mean that a black person can't get a job or be successful. It just means that race or racism is always there, lingering in the corner, waiting to show its face. The mere fact that your race is questioned on a job application is discrimination. What difference does it matter what my race is? I can understand questions about whether I am an American citizen or not, but my race? Still, most blacks looking for work can find a job.

It almost seems as if some were so annoyed that black people were free that they said, "Get away from us. Stay away from us." It was okay for black people to live in a white community as long as they were slaves and supported the master's family with their blood, sweat, and tears. The impact that abolishing slavery had on

American culture and social structure is amazing: "Since I can't own you, I'll burn crosses in your yard, kick your ass if you're caught here after dark, or shoot or hang you. And I definitely don't want you living around me."

Countless communities in the United States were designated as whites only, with signs in place to state this fact. For example, according to an article I read that was written by author James Loewen, Sand Mountain, in Georgia and Alabama, was an all-white community between 1890 and 1930, one of three thousand communities that expelled blacks during that time. Preston Hollow, a suburb of Dallas, was designated as an all-white area in 1956 by a covenant established by the neighborhood association. Though the covenant was ruled unconstitutional in the 1960s, it wasn't actually repealed until 2000.

During one of his standup routines, comedian Chris Rock described the community where he lives, a rich, white suburb of New Jersey. As a black man, he had to be a millionaire to live in the exclusive (and excluding) community, but his next-door neighbor, a white man, was a dentist. Black athletes and entertainers often represent the largest percentage of this type of integration. Otherwise, in my view, these overpriced and majority-white areas are off-limits to most blacks. As we say in my neighborhood, "If we can't be openly racist in the housing market, we'll simply price you out." I truly believe that single-family homes, condos, town homes, mansions, and other types of real estate are overpriced simply to keep those who cannot afford to own or rent them away.

I guess that's the American way: effectively determining who is or is not acceptable for a particular area. But I have to be honest; given the high number of dysfunctional and nonstructured black families in today's society, I can understand. I too want to separate myself from some of my neighbors. I would be devastated if I moved to a new area and my old neighbors moved in next door or across the street.

If you're black, being able to afford to live in a white community doesn't always mean that you're welcome there. I saw a documentary on former baseball player Curt Flood, which described the problems he endured buying a home during the 1960's in a designated non-black area in the Bay Area of California. The family of National Football League (NFL) quarterback Donovan McNabb was the first black people in a certain suburban community and had to endure racial effigies being left at their home. This was according to a story profiling McNabbs's career from his peewee days, and thru High School, College and the pros.

That's the way it is in this country, believe it or not, even though people may not like to openly discuss issues of race. For instance, the NFL doesn't have a black owner despite the so-called strides that have been made and the high number of black players who participate in the game. Indeed, I refer to the NFL, National Basketball Association (NBA), and Major League Baseball (MLB) as the good ol' boy network. My theory is that a select number of rich and racist white men draw the line at black people being invited to the table to eat with them(i.e., to own a team). Of course there are always those one or two token Negroes who may be allowed to join the network by paying the most money for a franchise in the history of sports, a record $2.6 billion, paid for by a group that includes former NBA star Magic Johnson, $1 billion more than the next highest price paid for a team.

As a descendant of slaves, I believe I am entitled to openly discuss race and racial relations in this country. After more than four hundred years of physical and mental enslavement of black people in America, the only choice I have is to be open and honest about the realities and perceptions associated with racial issues.

To speak about racial topics in the United States, I must first go back to the system that brought millions of black people to this country. Whether or not we like it, it happened, and every now and then we need to discuss it as it explains why many black people behave the way they do. I am not saying that we should live in the past, but the past has lasting effects.

During the trans-Atlantic slave trade, the Americans, British, Spanish, Portuguese, Dutch, and French captured West Africans; shackled, humiliated, and defeated them; then shipped them off to the colonies in North and South America. They were sold and placed at the bottom of the social ladder by torture, murder, and rape. The truth of the matter is most of this wouldn't have taken place if the slave traders were not aided by other Africans, who served as slave catchers, doing the dirty work for the colonizers. People hardly ever focus on this when they discuss slavery. Instead, most are taught to believe that white slave traders stormed the African coast and conquered and enslaved the Africans on their own. That is simply not true. Centuries before and during the trans-Atlantic slave trade, black Africans traded with Arabs: slaves were exchanged for goods. Between the years 650 and 1900, ten million to eighteen million Africans were enslaved by Arab slave traders according to the articles that I have read online when looking up the Arab slave trade. Obviously, whatever goods and money that were received by African tribes who caught and killed slaves during the slave trade, both the Transatlantic and Arab, were worth more than the African slaves lives.

The black African was the original sellout in my view and set the precedent for what was to come. It's almost as if this behavior was passed from generation to generation. Basically, black people got rid of their own, who suffered a fate that would change the lives of millions forever.

Mother Africa did not send any rescue ships, hunting parties, or helping hands to black people in America. The only things black people in this country received were lynching, castrations, laws in support of slavery and oppression, and depression. In reality, though, how many countries in Africa could have rescued anybody? They couldn't rescue themselves. The colonial powers didn't just capture slaves; they took over control of any area of value in sub-Saharan Africa. How much of that control still exists today? If you look up the countries that hold interest in Africa today you will find that the United States, Britain, Germany, Australia, China, and pretty much any other country taking pieces of the mineral-rich continent.

It's not like the fortunes of Africa improved after the slaves were shipped out. In some African countries, such as Sierra Leone, citizens murdered, enslaved, and tortured each other while the Western world profited from the diamond trade. Violence, famine, and corruption run rampant in Ethiopia, the Congo, Rwanda, and Burundi. The Mother Land is not so motherly, unless you're rich or an outside country benefiting from the continent's rich resources and the ineptitude of many.

One of the most troubling situations was in Rwanda, which was controlled by Belgium during the colonial era. The Belgians determined who was a Hutu and who was a Tutsi based on physical features, like nose and mouth sizes, skin color, and hair texture. The Tutsi were put in charge to run the day-to-day affairs of the government and were given good positions while the Belgians maintained control. The Tutsi, of course, feeling like the house nigger in charge, abused their power and mistreated and attacked the Hutu.

Before the Belgians gave Rwanda independence and left in 1961 they placed the Hutu in charge, which after all the abuse at the hands of the Tutsi, were vengeful and spiteful. The 1994 assassination of Juvenal Habyarimana, a Hutu and the president of the neighboring country Burundi, was a catalyst for the genocide in Rwanda that left 800,000 to one million people dead. Hundreds of thousands more were forced to live in refugee camps. The 2004 movie *Hotel Rwanda*, starring Don Cheadle, is based on this genocide. If we look up Belgium and its history in Rwanda in the encyclopedia we will find that the Belgians created more of an ethnic divide between the Tutsi and Hutu by supporting Tutsi power. Scientist believed that the Tutsis skulls were larger, and that the Tutsis had Caucasian ancestry and thus superior to the Hutus.

In Sudan, the Congo, and Uganda, civil unrest is not uncommon. In some countries, people have been slaughtered during so called ethnic cleansing; thousands of others were forced to flee to refugee camps. There always seems to be some type of liberation movement by one group or another during which hundreds of thousands are killed. In Darfur, Sudan, hundreds of thousands of black Africans are being killed by the Janjuweed, Muslims on horseback who are directed by an Arab Muslim government and military since 2003

In 1965, Che Guevara, the historic freedom fighter who aided Fidel Castro during the 1959 Cuban revolution, traveled to the Congo to prepare supporters of Patrice Lumumba for a takeover of their own government. Guevara noted that the black liberation groups were indifferent and could not agree on the best way to proceed to benefit all. According to the biography of Guevara, it was like they were having a revolution within a revolution, and were divided into two or more groups that disagreed with one another. His mission failed, and Guevara ultimately left Africa and returned to Latin America.

The kick in the head, though, is that, based on my personal experiences and what I have heard from others, some Africans here in the United States look down on black Americans. They believe that black Americans don't take advantage of the opportunities that exist in this country. How can anyone in Africa or from Africa look down on anyone in this country, when it was your continent that sold us? It was your continent that enabled this disaster to happen. You should be the ones who are looked down upon.

Who knows, if not for other African blacks I may have seen a lion, gorilla, or hyena in its natural habitat and in the wild not have to rely on a visit to the zoo to do so. I wonder if the descendants of slave catchers and killers are happy at what has been created and the aftermath that has followed since the slave trade?

Due to the corruption, chaos, and starvation and sub par living that exist in a number of African countries; I am in no rush to visit such places. If I did visit, I would like to go on a safari and view the animals, or maybe visit and view parts of Lake Victoria. Some may consider this a lack of sentiment for the African people; but I am simply stating my honest feelings on the matter. I am glad that I do not live in Africa, as bad it may sound. For whatever reason, it was meant for me to be in America, despite the fear and torture that awaited my people during and after the slave trade that still exist in some form today.

The role of whites in this disaster cannot be forgotten. The less-than-human conditions and torture on the ships as the slaves crossed the Atlantic is an epic tragedy. Shackled with corks in their rear ends to eliminate bowel movements according to a documentary I watched on the journey of African slaves to America, Black Africans were disgraced, humiliated, and broken. Women were raped on a regular basis, while the men, shackled, were helpless.

According to Antebellum Slavery economics, the twelve wealthiest counties in the US were in the south. Southern plantation owners and their families profited plenty from the trade. All those hate groups, like the KKK, Aryan Nation, etc., that think that black people are not entitled to be in this country should remember we didn't choose this country in the first damn place. They have some nerve to burn crosses, homes, and churches, to hang and castrate men, when it was your people who brought black people on a mass scale to this country.

33

You would think that for building this nation, making the South prosperous, and supplying white men with exotic women, we would get a "thank you, bro!" Instead, we get a burning cross and hate speech about how we should go back to Africa that this is the pure white man's country.

But while we chastise the white slave owners, we must chastise the black ones as well. According to articles that I have read on blacks who owned slaves, in particular Robert M Grooms via the Barnes Review; Justus Angel and Mistress L. Horry at one time owned eighty-four slaves apiece in South Carolina. In fact, in 1860 around 125 Negroes owned slaves. Some, like William Ellison of South Carolina, even paid white men to run down those who escaped.

I don't know what kind of syndrome or disease would persuade someone to do something like this. It must be the sellout syndrome or something like it, because what else could you call it? Black people have enslaved one another; it's a fact and a terrible one indeed. The black race seems to be in the business of selling each other off and out.

The government supported slavery; it was legal. Former President Woodrow Wilson was a segregationist who allowed *Birth of a Nation* to be premiered in the White House. The movie depicted the KKK beating and lynching blacks, who were really white actors with their faces painted black. Even if Wilson wasn't an active member of the Klan, then he was an accomplice and therefore a participant. Isn't it true that you are judged by the company you keep?

The 1910 Mann Act was created by Congressman Charles Mann, another resident of Illinois. The act made it a crime to cross state lines with a white woman for the purpose of paid sex or prostitution. The first person punished under the law was the first black heavyweight champion, Jack Johnson, who openly dated white women. I guess it's all right for white men to have their way with black women, but white women are too precious for black men. If you ask me, the Mann Act was the ghost of the past, representing the guilt of many white men who saw black women as sex slaves but were horrified by the thought of white women being sexual with black men. Such attitudes have existed since the slave era. Once slavery ended, the feelings of guilt and paranoia only intensified.

Jack Johnson was eventually sentenced to jail for his "crime" (i.e., taking a white woman across state lines and paying her for sex). The hatred that he endured for his boastfulness, for openly dating white women, and for his flamboyant lifestyle led to a ban on black fighters being eligible for the heavyweight championship. When they finally allowed someone willing to be humble enough and nonthreatening, Joe Louis, the anti-Jack Johnson, was allowed to fight for the heavyweight championship but only after an agreement was reached between Mike Jacobs, his promoter, and Joe Gould, the manager of his opponent James Braddock. The agreement gave Gould and his fighter Braddock a percentage of Louis's future earnings for ten years according to an HBO documentary profiling Louis. Did Louis have to sell his soul to be able to fight for the heavyweight championship of the world?

John Roxborough and Julian Black, Louis's early managers, were black men who did their part in toning down the fighter's image, advising him not to openly celebrate or boast when he defeated a white boxer. Louis was told to not have his picture taken with white women, which was seen as showboating and reminded many whites of the abhorred Johnson years. Roxborough and Black also cashed in on Louis, signing contracts that dedicated half of his future earnings to them.

It's no wonder that, after his fighting days ended, Louis's life was somewhat troubled. He had troubles with the IRS and was subjected to oppression and repression by both black and white individuals from the moment he stepped on the scene. Louis ended up a broken and beaten down man. What a heck of a price to pay for fame.

In my opinion, the Brown Bomber was and still is the greatest heavyweight champion. His twenty-five title defenses are unmatched. His accomplishments in the ring, his skill, his power are second to none. After his death, he was honored with a burial in Arlington National Cemetery. Louis probably was a great man, and I mean no disrespect to him or his legacy. But the facts are the facts. In the end, Louis sold out. Note that Max Schmeling, a German boxer who was defeated by Louis in 1948, was rewarded with a Coca-Cola distributorship in home country. He became a multimillionaire, while Louis was given hell and hounded by the IRS until the day he died.

It's because of acts like these and countless others that the United States needs to issue a formal apology to the descendants of slaves. Black Americans need to hear a public apology and an acknowledgement of their contributions to American society. A day of atonement, aired live around the globe, would help close the lasting wounds of slavery, at least slightly. The wounds themselves probably will never heal completely, but the broadcast would be a great move forward for both black and white people.

When you hear some say that "black people should get over it" or "it wasn't me or my grandparents who enslaved you," that is partially true. One shouldn't blame others because our ancestors were slaves, despite the fact some of those others are descended from slave masters and traders. You do have to move on, but maybe being told "we're sorry for over four hundred years of oppression and slavery" would ease some of the pains associated with being black in America.

Consider this. Most people whose ancestors were enslaved cannot tell you what part of Africa those ancestors came from. I don't know where my family originated; neither do my mother, father, grandparents, aunts, uncles, cousins, and friends. Who among us can say this but the black race? The Mexicans have Mexico; the Irish have Ireland; the English have England; the Germans have Germany, etc. I could go on and on. These races have a place to call home and, in some cases, a place to send money and where family members still live.

Black people didn't chose to emigrate to the New World; they were brought here by force. People of African descent, whether in America or elsewhere, have no reason to apologize about being black to anyone. Foreigners who migrated here more recently should be grateful for the contributions black people made to this country; otherwise, they can return home and be among their own people.

Recently, celebrities and others who can afford it have traced their roots back to their families' original country. I believe that this research should be done for every American with an ancestor who was enslaved and that it should be paid for by the US government. Every single black person in America deserves that, and none of us should have to put up a single dime. It is a small price to pay, considering what is owed to black people in America. After all, slave labor built this country!

Doesn't the slave trade warrant Holocaust-like status? Is the plight of the black man not equal to that of the Jewish man? Didn't the black race suffer permanent damage? Where is the compensation? Where is the reckoning? I am a supporter of the forty acres and a mule campaign. I am a supporter of reparations, which as Alan Keyes stated, should ensure that every working black American is tax-exempt for a certain number of years.

Jewish National claims against Germany made sure that the Jews were compensated for what they endured at the hands of the Nazis. In fact countries like Denmark, France, Italy, Bulgaria,

Austria and some others make payments to Holocaust survivors. They seem to have recovered quite well. It's not asking too much for the descendants of slaves to be compensated as well. Thirty to forty million blacks died during the slave trade according to Black fax, while six million Jews died at the hands of the Nazis. If I didn't know better, I might say this is a blatant example of one group being worth more than another group as well as of the racism and favoritism that have always existed in this country and in the world.

Tax-exemption and a onetime bailout of a negotiated amount is the last request I have for the US government. Along with an apology, it would go a long way toward improving America's image abroad. For example, in one documentary I watched on Dr. King during the middle of the Civil Rights era of the 1960's, Russia, who were engaged in a cold war with the U.S made mention of the fact that that the United States was advertised itself as the protector of the little guy around the world, even as American officials were spraying fire hoses and unleashing dogs on their own citizens. It would be a step toward healing, that is, if the United States is the country that it proclaims itself to be: a country that fights for freedom and democracy for others. It is time for the United States to come to the aid of black Americans in the same manner. The billions of dollars that the U.S spends on foreign aid giving countries like Israel and others could be used right here in this country.

Black Americans need to learn something once and for all. No matter how good or smart you may be, some will never see you as an equal. There will always be some neo-Nazi organization ranting that everyone who isn't white should leave the country. There is no need, in this day and age, to be shocked when racially motivated comments are broadcast on radio or television. Instead, people must teach their children to respect themselves and others, work hard, learn all that they can, and have faith in themselves and everything they do. They may meet others with different backgrounds and races who feel the same way they do, or have similar ambitions, and forge associations and friendships with them.

I am sick and tired of hearing people state their true thoughts about race and then backtrack later and offer a phony apology, usually to preserve a positive public image or keep a job. *I heard you the first time; you don't have to explain or apologize for anything.* In 2006, for example, Michael Richards, the actor who played Kramer on *Seinfeld*, went on a racial tirade against two black guys who had heckled him. He called them niggers and mentioned hangings. Audience members of all races sat with their mouths open as the racial insults spewed from Richards's mouth. The following year, radio host Don Imus referred to players on the Rutgers' women's basketball team as "nappy-headed hoes." Both Imus and Richards later met with black leaders and offered what I believe to be fake apologies.

There is no need to be phony when it comes to race. The experiences of black people in this country have been very real. Discrimination, lynching, beatings, torture, and police brutality are very real. There is no need to be shy, coy, or silent about issues concerning race. Maybe a race discussion or debate is necessary to ensure that all can state their opinions on the issue, particularly those who are afraid of being targeted or criticized. For all we know, everyone might be a racist in one form or another. A public discussion could help us find out why some feel the way they do about certain individuals or races.

Neo-Nazi groups often preach their rhetoric among their own members. But what if they expressed their feelings when their targets were present to debate the subject at hand? And no, cracking black jokes at work when there are one or two black employees present doesn't count as an open discussion on race. It's easy to crack black jokes when there are twenty-five white people present and only two or three black people, but it is not so easy when there are twenty of each group in the room. Then we would see how funny the jokes are.

Around the world, black people have been the target of physical attacks, insults, and stereotypes, including being depicted as monkeys or apes. The fact that black people have endured and survived despite this is a testament to the grace of God as well as our strength and perseverance. I'm willing to bet that every nationality has examples of people who, at one time or another, have referred to black people as "niggers."

But black people also stereotype and hold negative opinions of other races, whether or not they are true. We have always taken more than our fair share of insults. It's time that others heard our points of view. My intent is not to offend but to inform people about what black people say about other races.

> Jewish people seek to dominate the world, are greedy, want to control everything, and are oppressors of the black race.

> White people are crackers, racist but good at hiding it, corny, stiff, tattletales, crazy, and gross, and have no style.

> Mexicans are pepper bellies, spicks, suck ups, wannabe whites, snitches, terrible drivers, jealous of Puerto Ricans, and jealous of and hateful toward black people. Some accuse them of taking the place of black Americans, some without even bothering to learn the English language. Job Killers that bring about cheap wages for laborers.

> The Japanese are considered by some to be an evil race, kamikaze coordinators, elitist, and racist, "the white men of Asia."

Chinese people are called chinks or rice and dog eaters, slant-eyed, bad drivers, suspicious, and sneaky.

Arabs are sand niggers, all named Muhammad, disrespectful and hateful toward black people, and terrorists.

A race forum—an honest discussion about race with an equal number of white, black, Latino, Asian, and Arab people—would be interesting, if not helpful, in my opinion. The media makes sure that there are opportunities to form opinions about racial issues. Of course, issues within the black community are on public display every day. Many black people seem to enjoy being the jesters of the world, to entertain other races with their buffoonery. In fact, ignorant, uneducated, hate-filled, greedy, self-serving, and deceitful black people have made groups like the KKK and the Aryan Nations obsolete. Many black people effectively limit the damage done by these groups with their own behavior. Who needs hate groups when there are seemingly willing black people making sure that the black majority stays at the bottom of the social ladder? Some black or predominantly black communities only survive because of nonblack people who build rental homes and provide medical, and dental services that otherwise wouldn't exist in those areas.

The N Word
Recently the NAACP and others, including members of the hip hop community, decided that blacks should bury the N word. They even held a burial ceremony with a mock casket in 2007

Bury the word *nigger*? I don't know about that, and I'll tell you why. First of all, black people did not invent this word. It is a derogatory and insulting term used by other races to refer to black people. The NAACP and other groups should stop other races from saying nigger; until then, they're talking to the wrong people. Besides, aren't we dealing with enough problems already?

41

At this moment, some non-black is saying nigger this or nigger that to his family, friends, or coworkers. Someone who isn't black is telling a black joke. A white supremacist is speaking to a crowd or teaching his child the N word.

When black people use the word with each other, it has different meanings. When someone issues the greeting, "what's up, nigger?" that doesn't mean "hey, black dude," it means hello. It can be used as a noun to replace guy or person, as in "that nigger's good" or "he's a big nigger." Even when it is used in an aggressive tone or during a confrontation, it isn't always an insult. If I said, "Nigger, I'm going to kick your ass," the insult is me stating that I will beat you up, not that I am calling you a nigger, which is like saying dude or man.

Some black people are offended if they are called nigger by anybody, black or white. And they have a right to feel this way. We can't all agree on everything.

I have heard Latinos call one another nigger. Do they mean "black dude"? If I say, "That nigger Tom Cruise sure can act," am I saying that Cruise is a black man? Of course I am not. However if a nonblack person says nigger to a black person, well, due to the history of its use in that context, then that will and should be taken as an insult. It is offensive, ignorant, and a reminder of a dark period in history. It is associated with the past and current treatment of black Americans and will always be an insult when it comes from people who are not black.

Some say that black people empower the word by using it. How can this be? It wasn't the black man's word in the first place. Black people simply turned it into something more positive or at least less painful. What was an insult in one circle is not one in the other. This, in my opinion, decreases the power of the N word. It's only a word, but its power depends on who is using it and on whom it is being used. I assure you, black people are not keeping

42

this word alive. But we also can't bury nigger; it wasn't our word in the first place.

Some black people like to be called African American. Not me; my mother and father, and their mothers and fathers, and their mothers and fathers were born in America. As a race, we've been here for more than four hundred years. I've never been to Africa, so why should I place a check next to "African American" on a job application?

My people did not build in Africa; they worked their asses off, for no pay, in this country. Like it or not, with the exception of the Native Americans, blacks are as or more American than anyone in this country. The slave owners made that deal when they brought my people to the New World. Just call me an American, please, or black or colored, but don't call me an African American, thank you.

Race relations will never improve if only the oppressed ask, "Can't we all just get along?" The oppressors and offenders must be the ones to ask that question. Respect is earned and never given in this world; why don't more black people realize this?

In my opinion, black people can be racist only in theory and, as history has shown, we only oppress one another. How can you practice racism when you are the minority in both numbers and power? Black people simply aren't unified or powerful enough to implement practices or laws that negatively affect the lives of other races. A black person who does not hire a contractor because he is white, or fires a maid because she is white, might be considered racist by some. But those who believe in karma might see their actions as justified. When I hear white people speak about reverse racism, I instantly think of a privileged fool trying to convince the masses to believe a fairy tale.

CHAPTER 4

SEGREGATION VERSUS INTEGRATION

How did black people become one of the United States' biggest consumer groups, even though they are at the bottom of the totem pole compared to other races and represent only 13 percent of the population? Why is there not nearly enough black-owned industry to support our community?

One reason the black race lacks an infrastructure to support it can be traced back to the civil rights movement of the 1950s and 1960s. I believe that the events that transpired during that time helped shape the current state of black America.

A subject that often comes up during my conversations with others is integration, specifically whether it was good or bad for black people. Some agree with me that black people lost their independence and became dependent on others for their basic survival after integration. A common comment is that the lack of black businesses and entrepreneurial brothers can be blamed on integration. I can never figure out how being restricted from shopping in a clothing store or eating in a restaurant made people eager to shop there once the law said "now you can." If nothing else, it should have inspired an entire generation to become fiercely independent, determined to supply themselves and their people with their own medical centers, bakeries, and grocery and clothing stores, etc.

I sometimes think that black people who attempted to force and beg white people to accept them as equals acted out of sheer desperation. Jack Nicholson's character said it best in the 2006 film, *The Departed*: "If I got one thing against the black chappies, it's this—no one gives it to you. You have to take it." Marching with signs isn't "taking it" or earning respect; that's asking for mercy. And I thought only God gave mercy.

Guess what? We're still not equal, and that's because the law can't force people to change their feelings. An example of this is being served your food after white people sitting at another table even though they entered the restaurant after you did. As reported in a Newspaper article, a nightclub owner had instructed workers to keep black patrons entering, to make them wait longer for their drinks, or to play country music to make them leave. In the past you would always hear of young blacks complaining about not being allowed in a club because of the way they are dressed. Several years ago, a Chicago Bear football player was denied access to a club because of his dress style according to the news.

You can't force someone to accept or like you. Respect is something that you earn or take, depending on how you look at things. There are people that you encounter everyday in your own race who don't like you, so why should you care if individuals of other races think that black people are lower than dogs.

But given the way black Americans had been treated since our arrival in this country—the levels of hatred and violence to which black people were subjected—something had to be done. Many believed that the only way to survive was to integrate immediately. The civil rights movement was critical event in American history. Some of the groups and individuals who fought for equality and justice include the Black Panthers, and Dr. Martin Luther King

Jr. Sit-downs, protests, boycotts, and marches were prevalent during this era. Indeed, many of the rights enjoyed by blacks today are due to the struggles of people like Rosa Parks, whose refusal to give her seat to a white man was a catalyst for the 1955 Montgomery bus boycott.

The 1950s and 1960s were a turbulent time for black people in America, whether they lived in the South or the North. They were attacked for walking too far down the wrong street or being in the wrong neighborhood. In the South, they were denied access to restaurants and stores. In the North, they suffered political isolation.

Still, significant strides were. During the yearlong Montgomery bus boycott black people carpooled, walked, and even rode tractors rather than continue to be treated as subhuman on the bus. The racist bus company owners initially refused to give into the demands of the protestors. But after they lost hundreds of thousands of dollars, they eventually relented and allowed black riders to sit wherever they wanted. The Montgomery bus boycott was a major victory, an example of what happens when black people work together and of the power that unity has. The 1963 March on Washington in 1963 and the 1964 Voting Rights Act are other examples of what unity can do. With determination and sacrifice, gains can be made.

But as with most things, there are two sides to every story. Some mistakes were made within the civil rights movement. I believe that we came up a little short in our demands and settled for crumbs when we could have had more. How about some jobs to go along with those seats on the bus? When Dr. King had Lyndon B. Johnson's ear, did he focus more on getting funds for majority-black public schools like the majority-white schools received? Was Congress pressured into giving grants and other aid to black communities as it did with the white communities that we begged to join? If not, then why.

Integration in some form or another was going to become a reality anyway. Once black people across the nation built thriving and prosperous communities, they would have attracted the attention of others outside the race. It is the way that integration took place and the thought process of those who thought it was the only solution that disappoints me.

Did black people want integration simply for integration's sake? Did black people want to eat at a particular restaurant because the food was good or because we couldn't? I don't know if I would have wanted to eat at a restaurant that had declined to serve me the day before. How could I trust that my food was safe to eat? Was there an agenda, a purpose, a means to ensure the future of generations to come? Or was this just a case of we want it simply because we can't have it? We want to shop in this store simply because the owners won't let us?

This is what put black people on the path to being major contributors to the wealth of other groups by becoming the number-one consumer while neglecting our own needs and services. The only large money amounts that I know of that are spent by whites with blacks is crack cocaine and heroin.

Black Americans, people in who live in black communities, how many black banks are in your neighborhood? How many black-owned grocery and outlet stores can compare to a Jewel—Osco or a Kmart or Walmart? How many major black-owned construction companies are in your city or black-owned oil companies are in the Gulf of Mexico? How many high rises in your city have been designed by black architects?

John Johnson, founder of *Ebony* magazine, had the last and only high rise designed and built for a black man in America according to Johnson's bio. This is shocking, considering the strides that black people have made. Is one high rise all that black people can muster? You would think that we would have learned more after integration. Everyone can see what white people have done, but what does the black race have to show for it? Where are the skyscrapers that have been designed, paid for, and built by black Americans?

How many stretches of blocks have black bakeries, cleaners, donut and coffee shops, retail shops, and restaurants lined up door to door? Well, many white people have these types of businesses and can get most of what they need without leaving their communities. And if they have to leave their neighborhoods, there is a good chance that they can go to another thriving white community to get whatever they need.

There are a number of black-owned businesses in the United States, but not nearly enough to have an impact on American society. And, of course, all whites don't live in thriving communities; in fact, many are very poor. But white people are the majority, 64 percent of the population according to the latest census bureau. The poor whites can be covered by the successful whites, therefore averting the deficiencies in the white race that exist in the black community.

We hear constantly about high unemployment in the black community or black felons not being hired for jobs. Part of the reason for this is the lack of black businesses that could ease the burden of those looking for work. Instead, some black people have to depend on things like affirmative action or luck to be hired by a white-owned company, which is forced to hire a black employee because the law says so. How did we integrate a system, but not achieve the same results as white people did? If black people represent only 12 or 13 percent according to the census then there should be enough black industry and businesses to support them.

In 1921, Tulsa, Oklahoma, included an area called Greenwood. It was known as the black Wall Street because of its booming black economy—black clothing stores, banks, restaurants and doctors, dentists, lawyers, and oil men. White oil drillers who were out of work got loans from bankers on black Wall Street. Sadly, also in 1921 riots destroyed all of black Wall Street. An alleged rape or sexual attack of a white woman by a black shoeshine boy led to the formation of a white militia, whose members killed—depending on the account—anywhere from forty to three thousand black people. Thousands of others were held in barracks for eight days until a national uproar demanded their release. Most of the area was restored, but black Wall Street was gone and has never returned.

Survivors of the riots and some historians agree that integration played a major role in the area's failure to return to the commercial success it once was. Once black people were allowed to enter white establishments, the support was no longer there for the businesses of black Wall Street. What a shame. As we say in our neighborhood, "I guess the white man's ice is colder."

If more of us had the goals held by the black people of Tulsa before the 1920s, we could have achieved much more in the years following the civil rights movement. Forty years later, the same problems still exist: poverty, lack of jobs and education, and discrimination, minus the dogs and the water hoses.

In Chicago, 26th Street is a predominately Latino community that consists of more than a mile of Latino-owned business. It is second only to Michigan Avenue in terms of tax dollars generated for the city. Just like some white communities, Latinos have most of the services they need in their own neighborhood. They spend and build right in their own community, making it prosperous. As a result, they are commanding respect and gaining political power along the way. Latinos now have the power to make political and business moves that trump those of the black residents of the city of Chicago.

I do not mean to take anything away from anyone who was involved in the civil rights movement. Obstacles were overcome;

many black people became prominent and successful. All of that was great, but there is still much work to do. I believe that many black people didn't take full advantage of integration. Enough wasn't done to ensure that there was enough black-owned industry to support the community. These are areas in which the civil rights movement made decisions that benefited a few, but hurt even more.

In my opinion, black people could have gained much more by insisting on an equal playing field and continuing to pressure the government while laying the foundations for a black agenda. I have no doubt that the US and the state governments would have provided these opportunities if blacks insisted and were united, as was the case in earlier victories. The Montgomery bus boycott, the March on Washington, and the passage of the Voting Rights Act are great examples. Unfortunately, many in the black race asked for acceptance and nothing more than that.

I look around at the one-sided system that I was forced into by other black people. I don't see blocks with smoking stacks atop factory buildings owned by people who look like me. I don't see many trucks delivering meat that are owned by guys who look like me. In fact, I don't see even half the number of white-owned businesses or services under black ownership. Why did we beg for integration? I don't see the results, but I do see a lot of dependence.

What was the point of integrating when black people still complain of discrimination? I thought the goal was to be recognized as equals. Many become shell-shocked after going to college, getting an education, and becoming so-called successes when they are still treated as unequal. Hey, the white guys with signs reading "nigger, go home" were serious. They didn't want their kids going to school with your kids, to have you as a neighbor, or to give you that job or promotion.

Our needs and our children's needs should have been a goal; financial independence should have been a goal. Instead, years of dependence and inferiority have been passed down from generation to generation. Fear, dependence, and self-hatred have become part of the black DNA.

Some wonder why some white people believe that black people are inferior. Well, let's take a look, your honor. Basically, this is what integration said: "Black teachers can't teach black children, so can we send our children to white schools? We want white teachers to educate black children; they may do a better job than black teachers can." With this type of behavior, is it any surprise that some whites feel superior? Part of that blame can be placed at the feet of members of the black race.

A often-repeated joke describes how many black people are raised: they are told to go to school, get a degree, and get a job at a company. However, white people are taught to get an education, earn a degree, and then one day owns the company. Whether or not that is a stereotypical comment, it's painfully obvious that many white children get different instructions from their parents than many black children get. Luckily, I had a father and couple of older relatives who preached the importance of running your own company and being your own boss. But others I have encountered have encouraged me to settle and sell myself short; this is what I call communism talk.

From what I know and have seen, it doesn't take much to satisfy many in the black race. There is no need to give many black people bread to eat when crumbs will do just fine. Just look at the Fortune 400; currently the only black American billionaire on the list is Oprah Winfrey. One out of 399 is nothing to brag about, unless you're Oprah or her family and friends. Still, you hear some black people talk about her so much, you'd think she was the only billionaire in the United States. Of course, Oprah's accomplishments should be recognized and applauded, but who's next and who is after that?

We throw the word *equality* around quite a lot in America. But what is equal about it? Some black people will say, "at least we have Jay-Z, Puffy Combs, Magic Johnson, Michael Jordan, and 50 Cent." If you are satisfied with what you see, despite the increasing financial gaps between blacks and whites in this country, I have to ask if you are enjoying those crumbs.

Chapter 5

Social and Cultural Issues

Language

Bill Cosby annoyed some people when he addressed black people who abuse the English language. He ranted about how people embrace ignorance when they speak in slang, which continues when parents don't teach their children to talk properly.

I agree with what Cosby said. Ignorance and illiteracy are high in black America. Not since black people were prohibited from reading has the English language been misused and abused by so many. Far too many young people use the language of the streets, television, and radio. They get their English from rappers, videos, and their peers. I grew up in the 1980s, when you could get your ass kicked for walking down the wrong block or visiting a girl in a different neighborhood. In my community, gang-banging was prevalent, and tilting your hat to the right or left or offering the wrong handshake could lead to a beating.

But I have never seen as many ignorant and uneducated young black people as I see today. The lack of respect, negativity, and lack of principles has become so high that it is hard to talk to some young people about their behavior. You have to know proper English to be able to communicate clearly. Parents are responsible for the way their children speak and should correct them so they know which words or phrases to use or not use. But the youths themselves must take some responsibility for what they learn and how they use it.

Unless one plans on spending all of his life on the block, so to speak—which unfortunately is true of far too many young black males—it's important to be able to talk to anyone, regardless of race or sex. You want to be understood clearly, and you also want to understand the other person. I know some young black males who are quite content with not being able to socialize with those of different backgrounds. They have told me that they don't have to worry about interacting with other races because they're not leaving the hood anyway.

But those who do venture out into the world outside of urban America and the street will want to make an impression when they speak. You don't want to sound like you have no knowledge of the English language. Sometimes, you have to leave the slang and Ebonics at home. I'm not against Ebonics and slang when they are used in their proper place—with one's peers or in a social setting. Otherwise, turn them off and enter the real world. The problem is that many today are unable to turn them off because they only know one way to communicate.

Ignorant and uneducated parents raise children who are ignorant, and uneducated, and then they have kids, continuing the trend. The cycle is repeating itself over and over again in the black community at a rate that I believe will get worse before it gets better. Now we have a problem: too many young men and women with nothing to do and nothing on their minds. A recipe for disaster is being mixed up and spread in the streets of America.

If only the ignorant and uneducated fools would realize that knowing both proper English and Ebonics when necessary puts them at an advantage. Who knows what situation may arise, and knowing one language or the other could help in an emergency situation. There are classes on Ebonics. It's a part of American culture, after all. But the English language has been abused so much; it is having a lasting effect on society. It is understandable why an elderly and intelligent person like Bill Cosby would snap that black people need to abandon ghetto language.

After all, Bill Cosby produced one of the most positive and educational shows for black youth of all time. *Fat Albert* preached the values of going to school, staying away from crime, and respecting others. The show even featured a song at the end that reflected the theme of the day. Cosby also gave us a successful black family on television with a mother who was an attorney and a father who was a doctor in *The Cosby Show*. Many thought the show was unrealistic, because it included two professional and well-paid parents. That's part of the problem with American society: many don't see that black families can have both a successful mother and father, not even the black people themselves in many cases. Bill Cosby put a positive spin on black family life, something that was and still is needed. If he wants to complain about the behavior of black people, young or old, in my opinion he has earned that right and is correct in his assessment.

Music
I enjoy some rap music, but only old school rap from the 1980s to mid-1990s, the glory days. In my opinion, much of today's hip-hop is negative and damaging to black youths. There was a time when I thought people were insane when they targeted rap, blaming it for influencing young people, glorifying negative behavior, and inciting violence, robberies, and other crimes. But times have changed, and you'd have to be insane to believe that rap does not have a negative effect on young people. It has been especially damaging to black youth, particularly the songs about being a killer, mugger, or drug dealer. The black population is small enough as it is; the last thing we need is a lost generation caught up in a fantasy life. But that's exactly what is happening in cities across America.

Rap music used to have a message. A rapper would talk about how he woke up, took a shower, put on cologne, dressed, and got in his car. He would take you through his day. Some, like Chuck D and Public Enemy, KRS1 and BDP gave us history lessons and spoke about politics. They were what I call message rappers. "Fight the Power" and "My Philosophy" are examples of such songs.

Even gangster rap, performed by artists like NWA and Ice-T, was entertaining. These were guys who either had a prior street life, wished they did, or were describing those who did. Remember the outcry NWA caused when they released "Fuck the Police"? Or the stir caused by Ice-T's "Cop Killer"? Law enforcement, government officials, and others thought that they were inciting violence against the police. But black people have long been targeted by police, especially white officers, for beatings, unjustified shootings, harassment, frames, and overall mistreatment. That is no secret. So when NWA or Ice-T, who are black, said "fuck the police," they were simply venting and repeating the thoughts of many black people who are unhappy with the way they have been treated by the police.

In much of today's rap, there is too much bragging—about cars and their rims, jewelry, bankrolls, and women. These things are great, but how much focus can be placed on them before they become redundant? These aren't songs with meaning.

Young and poor people definitely don't need to hear today's garbage rap. Every other line is "you don't have this car, or these rims, and I do." What's a young and possibly naïve person supposed to do when he has no money, no rims, and no jewelry and keeps hearing this crap over and over again? Young teenagers should be focused on school, their friends, the prom, graduation, and preparing for the future. Instead, they are becoming materialistic and want high-end clothing, and expensive alcohol because rappers promote these things in their songs.

Negative rap, with its bad grammar and lack of meaning, is being banged into the heads of young people, and rappers have become their teachers. In my opinion, this is one of the major reasons the illiteracy rate is 44 percent and rising among young black people in this country according to a CNN poll. In fact the fascination with the hip-hop lifestyle and street talk about crime is the main reason many young black males and females are not interested in getting an education anymore.

Today, there is hardly any market for positive or message rap music. Negative and garbage rap is being promoted now, more than ever. Any meaningless song by artists with little talent is pumped through the airwaves, and we can see the effect on young black males and females across the country. A wedge has been drawn between young and old in terms of communication and respect. Rap music is the partial reason so many young black souls are lost.

The media accepts this garbage because it promotes negativity, puts black people in a bad light, and glorifies the bad side of black culture. In the end, it will set black people back even more. Take, for example, the Dirty South rap that is currently popular; except for acts like Outkast and maybe Jermaine Dupree, the lyrics are the worst and cannot compare to those of East Coast rap or artists like Common. But who wants to hear that? Today, it is all about negative influences.

Where is the balance that once existed in rap? Common raps poetically and somewhat politically. Lupe Fiasco covers controversial topics. I admire Kanye West's ability to tap into the crates, find and sample old records, and produce tracks that sound great. It's good that some rappers still do that, but their messages stink. What happened to songs like "Hey, Young World" by Slick Rick that encouraged kids to learn and respect themselves?

In the glory days of rap, we had more choices. There was gangster rap with acts like NWA, Ice-T, and Compton's Most Wanted. If you wanted sexually explicit songs, Too $Short and 2 Live Crew were your guys. If knowledge was what you were looking for, KRS1 and Chuck D were the ways to go. How about the smooth and earthy sounds that came from A Tribe Called Quest, De La Soul, and EPMD? During the glory days, we even had watered-down, college-style, or alternative rap. Rappers like Young MC, Tone Loc, and PM Dawn made popular and groundbreaking songs that stand the test of time. And who could forget MC Hammer and the style that he brought to rap? His baggy pants and awesome dance moves entertained many, and he was very popular at one time.

Today's hip-hop lacks variety, talent, and the sampling of old tracks to create a great sound. Some of the beats are almost demon-like. It reminds me of when some used to say that if you played heavy metal backward, you could hear the devil. I may sound old-fashioned, but in my view, some of the current rap songs are nothing but the devil's music. Rap music encourages negativity and confusion; the culture is sending young black people to jail and the cemetery as they follow along, lyric by lyric. In my opinion, it creates an environment that encourages young people to take the drug ecstasy, drink cough syrup and alcohol, and smoke weed. It's the only music that I know of in black culture—which includes jazz, blues, the Motown and Philly sounds, and soul music—that has a negative influence.

Where are the hot tracks? Some of rap's best songs were recreated with samples of a beat from another artist. Will Smith sampled "Summer Madness" by Kool and the Gang to create "Summertime," which became an instant classic. Rob Base and DJ E-Z Rock sampled Lyn Collins's "Think (About)" to create the song "It Takes Two." When Eric B. and Rakim sampled Dennis Edwards's "Don't Look Any Further" to create "Paid in Full," an all-time classic was born.

Today's rap artists seem to have a lack of knowledge and a disinterest in the music of the past like jazz, blues, rock, R&B,

and soul. Many don't appear to want to dig in the crates to give rap songs that soulful or jazz sound that we heard during the glory days. Maybe if more positive or laidback music was played in the clubs, fewer young people would be shot or killed while attending a party. Listening to James Brown or Smokey Robinson will not make you shoot up a club. Bad music and ignorant people are the reasons I stay away from most black clubs, especially where people under the age of thirty are present.

In many black communities, the blue-light special what some of the black elders called it, when love songs were played, giving young male and females a chance to get close, is a thing of the past. I can't remember the last time I heard a slow love song played in a club or at a party. Members of my generation sometimes would sit around at a party all night, waiting to hear a love song played so they'd get a chance to dance with the girls they had their eyes on. We wanted to slow things down and appreciate the special moments. Guys made tapes of romantic ballads that expressed feelings and love, be it young love.

Today, many young singers, in fact young black people in general, couldn't give a damn about older music and songs with stories, such as the blues. In Chicago, for example, go to a blues club, and you'll find mostly white patrons, from college-aged to middle-aged to older people. It seems to me that nonblack people have more of an interest in traditional black music than black people do. I once took a young lady who was around twenty-four to a live jazz club—an intimate, entertaining setting, with great lighting and good musicians playing good music. She didn't appreciate the music, the soothing and bopping sounds. She told me she wanted to leave.

Instead of inspiring people or making them think about different social issues, rap music has become demonic. Even current R&B songs don't seem to come from the heart or reflect the artist's personal experience. They are not songs with feeling. Today, music for young black is detrimental to their mental health.

I have no interest in contemporary R&B music. In my opinion, it is as bad as rap; it even sounds like rap. The 1960s, 1970s, and early 1980s—the Motown era and the heyday of soul and R&B—were the best decades for music for black people. "That's the Way of the World" by Earth, Wind, and Fire or "Walk on By" by Isaac Hayes contained nothing negative and made you feel good inside. Black music used to stir the soul, not influence young minds to be stupid; it used to inspire people, not help to destroy them.

It isn't inspiring to hear "I make dough, I move bricks" over and over again. It's downright insulting. This is what many young people are up against. The pressure is too much for them to handle, often with grave consequences. It's not acceptable that the financial gains of a few artists are deemed more important than the greater good.

Of course, you can't blame it all on the artists. The individual has to have some personal accountability. It's not up to the artist to make sure that a person can distinguish between a song and reality. It's narrow-mindedness and lack of sense and knowledge that is the real source of the problem. All I have to do is step outside, and I will hear some young brother quoting a line from a rap song about how he gets paid and that his bankroll is so big. I see children outside, ages ten and under, repeating the lyrics that they hear on the radio or television. Many young people do not understand that artists are trying to sell records and make money and will say anything to do so. Too many young people take what they hear and translate as literal and true.

However, hustling doesn't mean "sell drugs." It means working hard at whatever you do, whether it's washing cars, exterminating insects, or filing papers. To hustle is to do whatever you have to do to take care of yourself or your family. The lack of an education or self-awareness is causing hordes of young people to have minds of mush, to be easily misled.

It's no wonder black people continue fill up the prisons and the cemetery. They are chasing a lifestyle without acknowledging their own reality, living in fantasyland, and going to prison, where they are controlled by the establishment. Many petty criminals can't afford lawyers, can't afford to get out on bail, and couldn't show you $30,000 if their lives depended on it. That's hustling, all right. The acceptance and recognition of being incarcerated as a badge of honor has to stop. Prison is a punishment. It is not something to be proud of, because it means you were caught, that you failed. If a prisoner is blessed enough to survive his sentence, he should do his time, go home, and hope he won't return.

In the hood, you hear about who is going to prison or who just got out. Women talk about their baby daddies or boyfriends being in jail, the weekend visits downstate, and the money they either sent or didn't send. There are as many conversations about street guys in jail as there are about guys on the outside in some circles. You'd think that Don Corleone was coming home to take care of the family and make everything right.

Constant imprisonment is a form of slavery. Being told when to get up, go to bed, exercise, and communicate with the outside world is slavery. Even worse is the fact that hick towns now boom just like they did during slavery, providing employment through prisons as well as the restaurants and retail stores that provide even more jobs to the locals. It's another case of white men getting rich off the sweat of black people. If you are a repeat offender, then you are indeed a mental slave. For some, the only way to survive, the only way to be guaranteed a place to sleep and three meals a day, is to be imprisoned. Some people want to be told what to do. It's harder for them to survive in the outside world where there are responsibilities and pressures on a daily basis. Prison is nothing to be proud of and should not be worn like a badge of honor, which is becoming common in communities across America.

Far too many black communities are dominated by grime, ignorance, violence, and hatred. The dress code of the streets—saggy jeans, white T-shirts, and hooded sweaters—are signs of how neighborhoods are declining and how the financial gap between blacks and whites is widening. Many young men and women simply don't have an identity of their own; instead, they practice a form of self-hatred. When we were young, people of my generation liked to dress well, in dress pants and dress shoes. We sometimes wore each other's clothes, but we all had our own distinctive styles.

How did we go from suits and fedoras to saggy jeans, exposed underwear, and waistlines down by the knee? Young men wear no belts and have to hold their pants up with their hands, and that's cool, the in thing, and the norm. When crimes are committed, the police often give a broad description of the suspects' clothing: jeans, a white T-shirt, and a hoodie. Do you know how many young black males fit that description? The uniform gives the police free rein to suspect, arrest, and charge young black men with crimes that they may or may not have committed.

The uniform and the unclean appearance of many young black males makes both black and white people wary. It's not just nonblack people who lock their car doors when they see young black males approaching. Many black people, with good reason, are suspicious of the young black men they encounter in the street.

Maybe I shouldn't be so caught up in appearance, but grimy is grimy. There is nothing neat about saggy jeans and white undershirts; they're not sharp, and they look dirty. Furthermore, it does not reflect black culture, in which Stacy Adams shoes, dress slacks, gator boots, Dobbs hats, and sharp clothing run supreme.

Instead, no style and no class are being represented in cities across this country. Add in hatred, jealousy, and violence, and you have the ghetto today. The new trend of many young males wearing dreadlocks drives me nuts. Many who wear the dreadlocks don't wear them for religious reasons, like being a Rastafarian. No, they wear them because many are weak, are followers and have no identity of their own.

Groups of black people with different value systems living in the same area only add to the problems that confront black America. There are those who care and want to live a nice and comfortable life. Then there are those who don't give a damn about anything but partying, and destroying the property of others. There are those who stand around on the street corners in large numbers, loitering and littering, seeking attention as if they are working on the master plan that will save the entire world. Nonblack people who drive through black communities get to view a freak show. They go home with great topics for dinner discussions with their families and friends and even more reasons to not like black people.

Gentrification is taking place in Chicago. Public housing high-rise projects are being torn down. The projects were torn down because of the high crime that existed there. Poor and frustrated people were living in overcrowded spaces, the perfect breeding ground for drug abuse, drug sales, rape, and murder. The violence made police reluctant to enter without backup for fear of being shot from an open window or attacked in a stairway. The city grew sick of dealing with the bad press that followed some of the terrible crimes that took place in some of the projects and moved the residents elsewhere in the city and to the suburbs. The problem is that many people who grew up in the projects have a different value system than those in other communities. Disrespect, filth, violence, robberies, and murders are on the rise as people from different classes and social background mix it up. As bad as some projects were, they were at least isolated, in their own world some of them and able to be contained if the police did their jobs. Now they are in many worlds across the city and suburbs, and many residents are upset, terrified, frustrated, and fed up. Now Chicago is watched by the world and everyone is trying to figure out why the shootings and killings are as high as they are. Gentrification is leading to genocide in the black communities in Chicago.

The suburbs aren't as safe as people used to think. Bébé's kids have moved onto the block, and nobody is safe. The city and the police couldn't deal with the bad residents of public housing, but they are making the rest of society deal with them. You try to maintain a nice home; you cut your grass, shovel your snow, and are respectful. Your neighbor litters your yard with garbage and holds barbecues and parties in his front yard. His children and adult relatives trample your lawn. They behave as though life is a weeklong block party. He blasts music at all hours of the day or night, disrespecting those who have to rise early for work or school.

In some black communities, the streets are lined with garbage—empty potato-chip bags, paper plates, cups, torn boxes, wrappings from sandwich steaks. Litter in the street is normal to some people. If it weren't for the sanitation companies, cholera outbreaks would be common. I don't know why garbage cans exist in some areas because the people don't use them. There will be an empty trash can in the alley, and the garbage will be dumped on the ground next to it. Some people just don't give a damn.

Before many blacks can make it in the real world, they have to be able to survive the ghetto. Can you deal with the young men who park their cars on the street at 3 a.m., blast music, drink alcohol, do drugs, and eat food? Then they dump the trash right where they stand, in someone's front yard. It is common for gunshots to ring out at night and even in the daytime in many black neighborhoods in the city of Chicago.

Some are jealous of others who attempt to make better lives for themselves, labeling them as bourgeois or uppity. Instead of doing more to better themselves and their families, some would rather corrupt others and play the "misery loves company" game. For example, an individual comes into a large sum of money and shares the news of his success with his friends. Some of them are happy for him, for they know their lives may improve as well, or they are inspired to work to attain the same. Some aren't happy for him because he succeeded before they did. Still others take it a step further, and move to take what the individual has through force, robbery, or murder.

Forget about waiting until your time comes or being happy for the next person. Many want it now and don't care how they get it, even if that means taking someone else's possessions. People need to learn and accept that everyone's chances do not happen simultaneously. Everyone is different, born at different times and places. Life is the same way, but many have never learned how life works. Some will never succeed simply because they don't want to put in the work that is required to do so. Others don't succeed because they don't want to or because they are too busy worrying about what someone else has.

A couple grows up together. They both work hard; one or both graduate from college, or they become successful without a college degree. They have good careers and children and live the middle-class life. Another couple grow up together. They neither work hard nor take life seriously. They also have children. The second couple should not get mad or dislike the first couple because they have nice cars and their children are educated, well dressed, and cared for. Why should the first couple's children have to apologize because their parents worked hard to provide a better life for them?

The second couple chose to screw up. There is no need to say, "They think that their family is all that," or "she thinks she's something because she bought that car." Why not focus that energy on making life better for yourself? If you desire a nicer car and aren't in a position to have one, you have to wait. It may not be your time now, but it will be soon if you keep working at it.

You have to reevaluate yourself, educate yourself, try and better yourself. That way you can have some of what you want, maybe all of it; who knows? But you will never know by worrying about someone else. Each and every one of us has some business of our own that can be tended to instead of worrying about what others may or may not have.

Those who were born in poor families and had to do without should remember this: every wealthy family got its start with someone doing the work that was required to earn the riches. The Kennedy's are wealthy because their patriarch, Joseph Kennedy, laid the groundwork to make the family fortune, just as Henry Ford and John D. Rockefeller did for their families. Do not waste energy on being upset or concerned about someone else's wealth, whether it is real or perceived. If you want more, you must be a pioneer and make sure that your children and grandchildren have successful futures.

Imagine that a group of people are getting ready for a trip. They find out that the car is out of gas. One person goes to get gas, while the others wait by the car. Once the person returns they're all ready for the road. Someone had to get the gas, but everyone rides nonetheless. That's how it is. It's up to each individual to decide if he is going to be the one to get the gas or wait by the car.

In many black communities, other priorities have taken precedence. Other races joke about black people only wanting money to buy a Cadillac because the world knows that many blacks are materialistic. The poorest race continues to be the number-one consumer. This emphasis on spending much more than some can afford for fashion sakes is putting black people at an all-time low. Studies on poverty in America show that there is a $90,000-a-year gap in median income between blacks and whites. It seems to me that white people are making money while black people are spending money, money that they don't have.

It is true that there money was made during the crack epidemic that fueled the drug trade from the mid-1980s through the 1990s. But it came at a price. It destroyed many families across America, leaving many young men and women with no mothers or fathers to raise, clothe, and feed them. That money didn't beautify the neighborhoods; it destroyed them. The streets were filled with garbage, and people, young and old, were slumming on the corners all day and night in many communities. There wasn't a boom in construction; there was boom in destruction. All the while money was being made. Cars, rims, stereos, jewelry, clothes, sex, and splurging is all I saw, with only a handful actually making a real contribution to the community. While some focused on real estate, traveling, family, and the future, many couldn't see past the next flash in the pan. A slick car in the hood made you a star. You may not have had a place to live, just the car, but in the eyes of many, you'd made it. God forbid, you had $1,000 in your hand; then it was, "He got money, y'all. He's a baller."

It is hard for young, poor, weak, and naive young men and women not to be impressed by some guy who drives his new car in the neighborhood. Many of these ballers are afraid to go the areas where the wealthy are. They refuse to drive their fancy cars to high-end areas and park among the Ferraris and Lamborghinis and make it rain out there.

Why should I, or anyone else in the world, admire anyone who lacks the social graces? One may be a king in the neighborhood, but out of his element, away from the neighborhood, he is afraid and insecure. Yet uneducated individuals who are only able to survive in the ghetto and cannot handle the outside world are leading the way for the young in many cities in this country. These are the people who are glamorized in the ghetto.

The current fate of many black communities is a testament to the damage that was done during the crack epidemic. It not only destroyed the fabric of many families, but also left many young men and women chasing an era that their older relatives and friends experienced. The problem is that the surge has passed, that era is gone, but the damage is still here. All that's left is chump change, jail time, and death. Now black communities are experiencing the revenge of the crack babies.

To break the chain, black people have to go back to the old days. It's time to rebuild character. It's time for the young people to go back to the basics and earn money from jobs such as shining shoes, delivering newspapers, shoveling snow, mowing lawns, babysitting, and cleaning homes and businesses. Many black people seem to think these types of jobs are beneath them and yet these are ways of ending poverty and other ills affecting the community. Afterschool centers are fine; they keep young children off the street. But they alone won't solve the problem.

Some still face poverty and a lack of structure at home. To solve this problem, we may have to make young people work before or after school. Some may not agree with this idea, but what other choice do we have? The current system has failed. We can't keep making excuses, blame others, and continue to let the young suffer from the misfortunes or bad decisions of parents and other adults. Many Americans of all nationalities come from generations of hard workers with family values. There is nothing wrong with hard work. What better way for a family to grow together than by working together to make sure that everyone eats, sleeps, and lives comfortably.

Why wouldn't any young man or woman want to work to help take care of his or her family? It may be hard, but who said life was supposed to be easy? Some may have it easier than others in certain areas, but there are no guarantees for anyone. Besides, the odds of success for a young man who has the poorest background possible are extremely high if he starts working at a young age, learns the value of hard work, has his own money, and learns responsibility.

A thirteen-year-old who starts with a lawnmower and a rake on weekends may own a landscaping business by the time he is eighteen. Or perhaps the skills and experience he acquires will lead him to other business ventures. Or we can continue the current trend of 36 percent unemployment, with nearly half of young black people between the ages of sixteen and twenty-four unemployed according to the Center for Economic and Policy Research and wait to see how much worse it gets.

CHAPTER 6

THE POLICE AND THE JUSTICE SYSTEM

Whether anyone wants to believe it or not, racial profiling is a very real practice in the United States. Maybe people know it's real but just don't care, or believe black people deserve to be targeted. For some nonblack people, this experience could be so far from their reality that it's hard for them to acknowledge it exists.

Until you have had a firsthand experience, as I have, you cannot see how powerless being pulled over unjustly can make you feel. You don't have to break any traffic laws or have an expired registration to be pulled over. I have been pulled by the police over at least five times in the past 2 years; four of those times were random and without probable cause.

My father and other family members and friends also have been pulled over and treated like they were children and verbally abused, simply because they were driving a new Mercedes or Cadillac. These are men who worked nine-to-five jobs to support themselves and their families. The only law they broke was the law that prohibits driving while black.

Talk about the disparity. In Chicago, Cook County Board President Toni Preckwinkle supports making small amounts of marijuana less punishable by law due to most misdemeanor cases being thrown out, and overcrowded jails. In a study that followed it was reported in the Sun Times that Two percent of white people are arrested for possession of small amounts of marijuana while something like 86 to 90 percent of black people are charged with having the same amount. Latinos amount for something like 8 to 10 percent, according to the studies I've seen. Studies also show that while black people are targeted more often for possessing drugs in a car, pulling over white drivers leads to larger seizures of drugs.

Far too many times the police and the justice system remind black people that race is the primary identifier in their eyes. Those who have had some success and become wealthy are just rich niggers in the eyes of the law. I know that some black people like to believe that their degrees and their status place them in a different category. But lock yourself out of your house and try to enter through a window; one phone call from your white neighbor stating that a suspicious-looking black man is trying to break into the home will get you locked up. Everyone remembers when this was the case for Professor Henry Louis Gates.

That Gates and the cop who arrested him sat down for a beer with President Obama did not change the fact that many black people are viewed as nothing more than criminals. The law doesn't give a damn about how much education or money you have. In fact, your riches may actually work against you because of jealousy. If you are more successful than the cop who targeted you, he or she may hate that fact. And since the law is on their side, the cops can do whatever they want to.

Planting drugs, false arrests, and physical assaults are not uncommon. I believe that some people join the force hoping to get a chance to harass or harm some black person. I don't care what anyone says; my eyes don't lie. I know what I've witnessed.

How many times do we hear the suspect pointed a gun in the officer's direction? I'm not saying there haven't been cases where a suspect has aimed a gun at the police. But I believe that in most of these cases, the offenders did not point a damn thing at those officers, and that the mere suggestion that a black suspect is armed is enough to justify a shooting.

In some cases, no gun is present, and the offender is shot in the back. In other words, the suspect ran, turned, pointed something that looked like a gun, and was shot in the back? People who shoot at cops don't point guns; they shoot them. The suspect pointed a gun? That sounds like a game little kid's play. Who does that?

Of course at times policemen are shot by black suspects. Anytime anyone—police or suspects—is killed, it is not a good thing. Both families are sad and suffer tremendous losses.

When a suspect is shot or killed by police, the case often is closed pretty quickly; more often than not the officer's version of events serves as the final word. If a policeman is shot or killed, though, the judicial system makes sure that somebody will pay with a lot of jail time or the death penalty.

Who cares that a black mother is crying over the loss of her child because of an unjustified shooting? A weeping family of a slain officer though always seems to warrant a punishment whether or not there is evidence that the person charged with the crime actually committed it. Justice is demanded for the grieving policeman's family and usually given to them.

It's no secret that in many cases black people don't have the opportunities that many white people have in the law and the criminal justice system. How many times has a white person had his or her car approached by officers with guns drawn in a random traffic stop? In my opinion, whites get the benefit of the doubt and are afforded certain courtesies that most black people don't get. I've watched traffic stops in real life and on some on television reality shows, when a police officer pulls over a white person, the officer is verbally berated by the occupant of the vehicle and nothing happens. I've seen tickets torn up in an officer's face and the driver scream at the officer, who then tells the driver to have a nice day.

It isn't just white cops who abuse black people. Black cops, perhaps eager for respect that they didn't receive when they were kids or wanting to show off for their nonblack fellow officers, will bust someone's head, pull his gun, and even shoot a suspect. Latino policemen exhibit an "in your face" and aggressive attitude toward blacks in many cases as well, especially in Chicago where, in my opinion, most of the Latinos in positions of power or authority are the same or worse than the racist whites.

Most other Americans probably don't believe that this type of behavior exist within the police. Many probably hear about cases of police brutality and think that the "criminal" deserved it or was lying about being unfairly targeted or physically harmed. I mean no disrespect to the good cops out there; I have encountered some police officers who were quite helpful and positive. Of course all cops aren't bad ones, but the bad ones are out there, and you know it only takes a couple of spoiled apples to ruin a bunch. That's the way it is. Truly, being a policeman is a stressful, trying, and dangerous job, and I am sure some are doing the best they can and are genuinely good people.

But I believe that others are deliberately carrying out a agenda, a personal vendetta, or grudge against a certain group of people. It makes me wonder what type of department or organization would hire people with these types of attitudes to serve and protect others. Actually, I don't have to wonder because I already know what type of people would hire racist officers. There are stories about police harassment and brutality in Los Angeles, Oakland, New York, Chicago, Cincinnati, Atlanta, Georgia, Miami, and anywhere in the United States where blacks reside. Is this a coincidence, or is it the American way?

The police who patrol the streets in the black areas in my city seem to be more interested in targeting those who don't wear a seatbelt or in making sure that vehicle registrations are up to date, although these are areas with open drug sales and loitering on public property. Some officers would rather harass and target regular working men, the men with things to lose, than to go after criminals. I guess it's easier to bully honest and hardworking black citizens than the crowds of young black criminals on the corner. I have been randomly pulled over several times after work and on my way home. On several occasions I was pulled over near a drug corner where gentlemen were openly selling drugs. Yet, I was the one being harassed.

To some degree, the police are a legalized gang. They seem to roll in numbers and gang up on individuals just like gang members do. They also seem to get away with these tactics with little or no consequences. It never surprises me when I hear a report about a corrupt police officer. From what I've seen, the police can get away with harassment, violence, and murder simply by making up a story. And when they are backed by their fellow officers, it only makes sense that some officers would feel untouchable and able to get away with anything.

I have concluded that most police officials don't care about black people. They are here to serve black people with harassment, racial profiling, brutality, and murder while they protect the white community. Certainly, black people aren't being protected. In what some call the two-for-one deal, many black people, including me, believe that the police don't care when blacks kill other blacks. They will arrest a suspect only when the crime kills two birds with one stone—when one black man is dead and another is jail for a long time, effectively ending his life as well.

So what is the role of the police in the black community? If white neighborhoods start experiencing high levels of violent acts against their citizens, you better believe that there will be a stronger show of force by the police in those particular areas. Yet black people aren't afforded this right, despite high crime in their neighborhoods. It is blatant discrimination and a reminder of what the real role of the police in black areas: containment. How would white Americans feel if their neighborhoods were patrolled by predominately black police officers? What if those officers behaved like black militants, like the Black Panthers?

The Black Panthers mobilized, armed themselves, and patrolled their own areas in the 1960's. They policed the police, who were there to oppress, harass, and brutalize the residents and not to protect them. It's the same now, and it's time once again to do something about police brutality. I, for one, think it would be great if an independent security force to protect black areas was created. The police force could continue protect the interest of the whites as it always has and leave black people alone.

Jack Cover, the late physicist (I might call him an evil, mad scientist) who invented the inhumane Taser that the police use, should have been tased over and over himself to see how it feels to have high voltage running through his body. The Taser sends high-voltage shock via prongs to immobilize a person. There have been several cases of individuals dying after they were tased. In some cases, the reason given was that the victim had drugs in his or her system. Does that mean the person deserved to die? Maybe they would have slept off whatever drug they were on if they had not been tased.

What about people with medical issues? Are people like cattle? There are people in this country who complain about the way animals are killed to produce the food we eat, but humans are allowed to be tased and slaughtered. I saw the owners of Taser International on an episode of 60 Minutes in 2011.3 They were, of course, defending the use of Tasers by police since their company has cornered the market and makes millions selling the weapon to police departments across the country. The report questioned whether police were too quick to use the Taser rather than trying other options to control a suspect. The Taser makes a police officer's job that much easier, even though it turns the general public into guinea pigs and experimental laboratory rats.

The inequalities of the justice system are nothing new in America. An innocent black person will go to jail for a crime that he didn't commit, and white people will be acquitted for murders of black people. The justice system seems to favor whites, from my standpoint. There is nothing that exists that makes me believe otherwise.

Racism runs rampant in both police departments and prosecutor's offices. Anytime there is crime committed by a black person, especially if the victims are white, someone's going to be arrested whether he is the right person or not. Thankfully, with the introduction of DNA tests and work from college professors and students, some justice finally has arrived for those who have been wrongly convicted. As a result, innocent people have been released from prison, some after serving lengthy sentences of twenty years or more.

Occasionally, the wrongfully accused have been compensated, sometimes with millions of dollars, for their time and suffering. It's great to have the money, but nothing can give back the time, people, and ties that were lost. How do you make up for the loss of their children's youth? Some former inmates can't adjust to the outside world that they know nothing about, and end up returning to prison after their release. They have become institutionalized and broken, like a slave.

A moratorium on the death penalty in Illinois was enacted by former Gov. George Ryan and put into effect in 2003. This put executions on hold in the state, to the dismay of many. I guess there are people in Illinois who would love to continue the execution of people who might be innocent, especially if they are black or Latino or the victims are white. Citing the Death Penalty Information Center, of those sentenced to death, 77 percent of their victims were white, while only 15 percent were black. What does that tell us about whose life is more valued in this country?

I support the death penalty if the convicted person is the right person and if the criminal act was heinous. But the system is flawed and biased. Since 1973 there have been more than 130 wrongly convicted individuals on death row according to Amnesty International USA. Who knows how many wrongly convicted people have been put to death. Since the justice system is unable to apply the laws correctly and fairly, it may be time to end the death penalty in the United States of America.

In 2011, the moratorium placed on the death penalty by Ryan was finally made official by current Illinois Gov. Pat Quinn. It's a great accomplishment in my eyes, and I applaud Ryan tremendously. His effort was worthy of the Nobel Prize. Ryan was convicted of corruption in 2008 and was sentenced to six and a half years in prisons. He has been denied an early release on several occasions and is being punished unfairly, I believe, because of his death penalty moratorium and the subsequent release of black inmates. Many residents in Illinois, which is one of birth places of the KKK, which was established in Southern Illinois in 1875 per an article I read written by Dr. Andy Hall, are mad at him because of this. The sad part, though, is that no blacks made any public pleas for his release. Where were the protests and public pleas by the men and their families and friends who were affected by Ryan's decision to grant early releases to prisoners?

To some black people, justice has become "just us." It seems that those being served by the court system are mostly blacks serving prison time. Black people in prison are creating economic booms in towns that would be nothing without the prisoners who create jobs for many. Many of these towns have people who don't even welcome black visitors. But they all experience the growth that the prisoners provide. It's a modern day slave trade; once again whites are getting rich off the black man's blood, sweat, and tears.

In several high-profile cases—like Michael Jackson's trial for molestation or R. Kelly's charge of sex with a minor—the accused escaped jail time. Those occasions are far and few between, as most prisoners are not rich and famous. They won't avoid jail time. O. J. Simpson, one of the luckiest and dumbest black men of the century, beat the system and then flaunted it in the faces of white people. He continued to get in trouble with the law and even wrote a book titled *If I Did It*. White people and the law couldn't wait to get their hands on him again and send him to jail.

O. J. had been around white people so long that he felt that he was as privileged as they are and that he was untouchable. He was so out of touch with reality that when he did decide to hang with some brothers, they turned out to be rats who sold him out and cooperated with the government in convicting him. I can still see them, black guys dressed sharp and trying to look cool, all the while being nothing more than overdressed stool pigeons.

O. J. was considered guilty before he came to face his attempted robbery charges, and everyone knew it. There was no way he was going to escape prison a second time. I know how it goes: with an all—or predominately white jury, your ass is out; you are guilty. In my opinion, the only reason he got away the first time was that the white racist cops were overzealous in their investigation. Had the cops put their hatred of black people aside for a while, Simpson may have been found guilty of the 1994 murders. Instead, his acquittal sent shock waves through the white community and celebrations throughout the black community. The real America was exposed; white America was so annoyed and didn't stop talking about his being found not guilty of murdering

Nicole Brown Simpson and Ronald Goldman. Ten years after the murders, talk show hosts continued to talk about Simpson and the murders. White America simply never let it go. Talk show host Jay Leno and David Letterman included an OJ joke or comment every month it seemed.

Many black people celebrated him being found not guilty. That was not because they liked O. J.; most could care less about Simpson and considered him to be an Oreo or a white nigger. But in the minds of many he was one of the few black men to beat a major charge and not be hanged, so to speak; that was a reason to celebrate, whether or not O. J. was an Oreo.

The behavior of some whites after his acquittal was interesting to say the least. Reminds me of the old plantation south days when you would hear" How dare this coon touch that pretty white lady and get away with it" And everyone knows that when white women are harmed, justice will be served in America. Only in cases where powerful and wealthy white individuals have committed harmful acts toward white women will justice falter. If a black man harms a white woman, there will be a hanging for sure, whether the right suspect is charged or not.

If a white woman murders her children, she must have been insane, because there is no way that a white mother in her right mind could kill her child. However, a black woman who murders her children will go to prison; the courts will not accept any insanity plea offered by her legal counsel, that's for sure. In Florida, Casey Anthony was charged with killing her baby in 2008. She was tried in 2011 and would have faced the death penalty if she was convicted. But she was, of course, acquitted. A white jury will not send a white woman to the death chamber without an overwhelming amount of evidence.

The best advice that I can give young black people about the justice system and law enforcement is to try to stay away from them, if possible. "It won't be good for you," I tell them. The system is crooked; the juries are loaded with predominately white racist jurors who are looking to screw up your life. The jury-selection process is administered by a racist system that places your life in the hands of racist individuals.

You had better hope and pray that you're never framed for a serious crime. If you're black you will not get justice, you will find *just us*!

Chapter 7

Parents and Crime

There is a problem in black America, one that is so detrimental that if it is not dealt with, it will play a major role in determining our future. Childbirth rates among middle-class blacks, those who can afford to care for a child, are on the decline. They are being overtaken by the poor, the uneducated, those being cared for by the government. To put it plainly, the wrong people are having babies, while others are more focused on their careers, themselves, or on dating the same sex. Since only 13 percent or so of the American population is black, at the rate that things are happening now, the black race as we know it could be headed for the museum, as an exhibit in the future.

An unhealthy amount of black babies are being born in the ghetto to parents who have nothing positive to teach them. Too many ignorant, disrespectful, and tacky black males are ruining the lives of young black women, some who are just as disrespectful and tacky because they have nothing to offer or teach them or their children. Then there are the young and uneducated black women who date and have children by these clowns. This cycle is repeating itself in many ghettos across America.

Bébé's kids are on the loose America and are coming to a neighborhood near you. The crack cocaine epidemic that tore apart the fabric of many families has all but destroyed many black families and communities. Many would-be fathers and mothers became addicts or dealers, and as a result slaves for the penal system, heading toward a wasted life or early death.

Addicted mothers left the raising of their children to the street. Children of the drug epidemic are in the street in high numbers, and since no one gave a damn about them, they don't give a damn about anything. What except despair and negativity can be expected for the child's future when his so-called parents are more concerned with putting on saggy jeans and cocking their baseball caps to indicate their gang affiliation?

So many negative influences for young black children wait outside their front doors. Only the strong survive in the ghetto. It's a cliché, but it's very true, because on almost every corner in some neighborhoods, there are petty drug sales and unemployed men and women who sit around all day and night, doing nothing besides getting high and drunk. Some take what they learn from the street, apply it to the real world, and learn how not to behave. Others become victims of the streets—poor, drug-addicted pushers or bums who hang out with the wine heads on the corner. High numbers of young people are so affected by the poverty and negative influences around them that preying on the community becomes a way of survival.

Many black mothers and fathers have failed and are failing to raise their kids. Undisciplined children are the norm far too often in the black community. Too many young black people are becoming the world's burden because someone didn't take on the responsibility of teaching them a better way of life. Sometimes, even children who have a typical two-parent upbringing or a strong one-parent upbringing decide to become losers and criminals. So it is twice as likely that those who don't receive proper instructions will become negative influences.

There was a time when discipline existed in the home, on the block, in school, and in church. Much of this has disappeared today and at time when a belt on the rear end is needed in many instances. What happened to spoil the rod, spoil the child? I am not talking about the idiots you see on the news who chain their children to radiators or lock them in cages or in basements, or the idiot who breaks his six-year-old son's neck for eating a roll without permission, or the boyfriend who beats his girlfriend's baby to death, or other violent acts committed against children.

Some black people blame the lack of discipline on white-run organizations like the Department of Children's Services, saying it wants black people to lose control of their children. In the old days, black people didn't give timeouts to their children; they whipped them, and their kids turned out all right. Children have no reason to fear their parents anymore. In recent years, you even hear about black children murdering their own parents, which was never the case in the past. Your own child, who you bathe, feed, and clothe, can call the police on you to avoid being held accountable for his actions. What is the world coming to?

When spanking is order, parents should do so. Some call spanking child abuse. It is true that spankings or whippings, which is what they were called in my day, are not effective tools for all children. Some children can be disciplined with words and punishments. But there are some, as was the case with me and almost every other kid I knew, who simply didn't believe that fat meat was greasy, and being whipped or pinched or smacked helped us to realize that it was.

Comedians and others joke about white kids throwing tantrums and embarrassing their parents in public places. Then they'll describe a black mom who embarrasses her child with a yank or a smack in the head—a reminder of what not to do next time. In my day, if a child embarrassed his mom, the one who birthed and cared for him, in public, he'd end up being the one embarrassed.

Many in my generation couldn't even say the word *lie*; we'd have to say that we were telling a "story." A lie was considered the equivalent of cursing or swearing, and if you cursed at or around your parents, you'd get a smack in the mouth. Some children did talk back to their parents, though not as much as the white kids did, or so we thought. Talking back was something you did at your own risk; if you were lucky, you were chastised (i.e., "checked by your parents" with a nice verbal message), or you were smacked.

Your neighbor might have pinched you if he caught you climbing his fence or entering his yard without permission. When you ran home and told your parents, they'd say that you probably deserved it or that you'd better respect the neighbor. In school, teachers weren't afraid of students. Gangbangers and everyone else knew that teachers would grab a hold of them and ruff them up if they disrupted the class or were unruly in the hallways. I recall one gangbanger in grade school challenging a teacher to a fight on the playground. When the student got ruffed up, his mom didn't call the police or go to the school and complain. Neither did the gangbanger. They knew that he deserved it because he had behaved terribly.

When the ruler or the pointer were used, or when collars were grabbed, it was seen as punishment for wrongdoing, not as child abuse. You screwed up, you knew it, and you accepted your punishment. That was it. Nowadays, the only corporal punishment that's dished out in school is when students physically harm the teachers. If a parent hears about a teacher or a coach putting his or her hands on his child in this era, odds are the police will called and the teacher accused of abuse. The offending student will be seen as a victim and not the instigator.

Metal detectors in schools—who ever heard of such a thing? Kids aren't stupid; they know that they can get away with almost anything without the worry of any corporal punishment in most cases. In effect, there has been a switch in the balance of power, with the odds clearly in favor of the unruly kids. In fact, some disruptive youths' first encounter with accountability and consequences are when the police are involved. By then it is often too late, depending on the severity of the act that was committed. Despite a smart mouth, misbehavior, and disrespect, a child's first smack in the head may be from the law, which won't be acting out of love, I can assure you.

My peers and I were held accountable for our actions and punished for our mistakes. We turned out all right because people gave a damn about us and wanted us to succeed in life. Even those who didn't get their acts together and continued on a path of destruction understood that they were accountable for their actions. Today, many will tell you how they screwed up and should have listened to what Mom, Dad, or the math teacher were saying all along.

Today, there is no one to hold many young people accountable. On a regular basis, I witness children, aged anywhere from six to thirteen, misbehaving, throwing rocks at neighbors' cars, swearing in the presence of adults. Today, though, one has to be careful about correcting a neighbor's kid for unruly behavior. Many of the parents are unruly themselves, and they ask, "Why are you interfering with my child?" rather than addressing why a six-year-old is cursing in the presence of adults.

The values and education we learn as children remain with us throughout our lives, even those of us who do stupid things. Individuals may decide not to heed the advice of their parents or other adults; for whatever reason or excuse; they will go down the opposite path and choose a life of destruction or despair. I've had conversations with those recovering from drug or alcohol addiction or lives of crime, and they say that the biggest reason they overcame their obstacles was the strength of their families. They weren't applauded for their bad choices; they were scolded and reminded constantly that there were options other than the crazy things they were doing.

Many in my generation had positive male role models. There were Fathers and uncles, cousins and friends, and neighbors—men in whom a kid could see alternative ways of living. These men encouraged success; they preached about getting an education, earning a good living, making money, and buying property. They warned about the consequences that would follow if you did not prepare yourself for the world. These men spoke out against going to jail, being a bum or poor, or having no plans for the future.

The women—mothers, grandmothers, aunts, and other female relatives—made sure that the children knew about going to summer camp, the zoo, museums, the movies, or the park to have fun. They made sure that you were properly fed at breakfast, lunch, and dinner. They also disciplined you when you were wrong. Aunt Betty wouldn't hesitate to pull your ear or pinch you when you acted up.

People need to hear more stories about how moms and dads worked hard or how grandma helped ensure that kids had a chance at a bright future. It will take more than the "I'm living my life" statements that come from some women to save this sinking ship. If you are single and without children, then party all day and night if you choose. But those young mothers who stay in the club or in the street, chasing this person or another, leaving the child or children behind at grandma's or another relative's house on a regular basis, have to stop. Sometimes mama and grandmamma are both at the club, partying together.

Children are being born to unprepared, dependent mothers and fathers who are unwilling to make the sacrifices necessary to raise the children that they have brought into this world. Without a strong family, where will the child go? Many are trapped in a world of negativity, suffering, and despair and are vulnerable to the influences of the street. Many aren't strong enough and surrender to the evil forces that surround them.

My father often preached about the importance of sons being more successful than the father. Whether that means financial success, the expansion of success, or an innovative contribution to society, striving to be better than your father is inspirational. Even if you never become as successful as your father in one particular area, your success can be attained in another one. Failing is not an option in this plan, because your aim is to do better, not worse.

Those with fathers who are unemployed, drug addicted, or underpaid or simply weren't there for you also can strive for certain goals. These goals include being a better man than your father. It might be easier for some than for others, depending on how good or bad your dad was. Many of success stories are associated with those who had humble beginnings and a troubled or deprived childhood.

In some cases, the biggest obstacles for many black youths are the people who surround them. The number of black men and women who are ignorant, unintelligent, uneducated, and unemployed in today's society is high. Unless young individuals are shown an alternative lifestyle, there will be an ongoing cycle of negativity in which the disorderly and backward way of life becomes the norm and even an accepted way of life in black communities. That is exactly what happened to the children of the crack epidemic—poverty, violence, disrespect, rundown and garbage-filled blocks have been passed on, creating a generation of losers, many with no hope for the future.

The term "born loser" is very real. There is truly such a thing as being born into the wrong family—one with ignorant and unsuccessful parents, grandparents, uncles, aunts, cousins, friends.

A child born into such a family has the deck stacked against him from birth. Some will never escape, and they are the ones who threaten and tear down already fragile black communities. These rotten apples are the reason vigils are held in cities across the country to stop young people from killing one another; they are why conferences on crime are held. Still, many beat do the odds and go on to have a productive, meaningful, successful lives.

Are we prepared to deal with the aftermath of the crack epidemic? Obviously the answer is no, because we are losing the battle. We the public, especially those who live in areas with high crime, have become prisoners in our own neighborhoods. People are afraid to walk to corner stores because of the young people loitering around and crowding the entrances. Incidents of rape being committed by young black males, eighteen years old or younger are being reported on the news and in the papers in numbers that I have never witnessed. Home invasions and the robbing and attacking elders are up as well. It seems to me that violence and hatred are at an all-time high in black communities.

It is not enough to simply lock up the repeat offender, nor is that an effective way of stopping the crimes. You lock up one punk; there will be another to take his place. In cities where gangs are present, jail is a reward; it is where the other gang members are. It is where one can achieve higher ranking in their particular gang. It's like being on the street but with three meals a day and the availability of exercise equipment, snacks, and camaraderie. Jail is a second home to some, a place to escape the cold winters rather than a punishment.

You know what punishment is? Sending first-time and repeat offenders, guilty of murder and robbery, to the military and having them pay their debt to society by defending the country that they harmed. Sentencing an eighteen-year-old to seven years in the military would be a more effective way of punishing and rehabilitating a criminal.

The military is where young men can be disciplined, trained, taught respect, and in some cases even honor. The current penal system does not rehabilitate most inmates. The military—boot camp and deployments overseas—do. If an offender continues to be disruptive during boot camp or service, a prison sentence could be the next option, of course. Let's hold these offenders accountable, whether they are black, white, Latino, Asian, or whatever. Sentencing criminals to military service would be an effective tool and would cut crime in half instantly.

How many choices do we have left? Do we sit back until most young black people are dead, either by the hand of another young person or the police?

The system would have to be fair of course, and that would be my only concern. The police accusing and locking up the wrong person is always a concern, particularly if you're black. We cannot have racist juries or judges deciding the fate of any more black youths. A jury of the offender's peers, meaning that at least half of the jurors are black if there is a black defendant, is what is needed. We don't want an innocent man to be convicted simply because he was at the wrong place at the wrong time.

Since they say this is an equal-opportunity country, the females who imitate males and commit serious crimes, like robbery and murder, should be enlisted as well. They too can protect the interests of this country and pay their debt to society.

For any society to exist peacefully, for a community to prosper and build a future, a certain degree of order has to be in place. Those who prey on and destroy the community have to be contained; otherwise, how will we build and succeed? It's time to rebuild for the babies who have yet to be affected by this terrible pattern of demise and destruction.

Parents or guardians should raise their kids so that no one else has to. There are parents who do take care of their children, and their kids choose to be an incorrigible just because. That is not the parents' fault. The child made the decision to go the opposite way.

It's time to confess about the problems that plague us, to clean up and move on. Those who aren't holding their weight should be called upon to do their part. Otherwise, they should get out of the way; let the government take care of them, while they sit on the sidelines and watch.

The hood needs to stop corrupting young people and give them chances to make something of their life. The way I see it, no one can force anyone to do the right thing; we all have been given free will. If an individual wants to destroy or waste his or her own life, then so be it. But why bring others down or take innocent people into a less-than-ideal existence? Sink alone, waste your own life, and leave others alone.

In my youth, the wine heads told us stay in school, and do the right thing. Even some of the gangbangers respected those who attended school, minded their business, and lived their own lives. The black community as a whole didn't prosper from the crack epidemic; it crashed. The young need to be reminded that the high-incarceration rates facing blacks today is a result of the crack era and were not worth it. For the temporary gains of a few, many black families and communities have suffered, and lives have been destroyed, some permanently.

Based on the "good times" I see in my community and in my city, as far as black folks are concerned, we're getting money and making it rain. You wouldn't know that times are bad; the celebrations would lead you to believe that all is good in the hood. In fact, the opposite is true; things are at a never-seen-before low, and they're getting worse every day.

CHAPTER 8

ATHLETES AND SPORTS

My earliest introductions to sports were of the best being the best. Whether it was boxing, football, baseball, or basketball, I was treated to championships and athletes striving for the best. Even those who lost did their best; they just weren't as talented or tough as those who achieved titles.

Today, championships are still being won, but with the exception of baseball I don't feel as though I am watching the greats. I believe that mediocrity has become the norm to some degree. Consider the number of dropped balls in the NFL and the bad plays and terrible teams in the NBA; even I could do better. I never thought I could be as good player as Isaiah Thomas or Jerry Rice. In the "make it rain" era, many in the NBA and NFL are overpaid and not earning their keep as professionals.

My memory of sports goes back to somewhere around 1977 or 1978, and my interest started with boxing. I watched it on television, and then I heard the name Muhammad Ali. I was hooked; I became a fan of Ali right away. I recall the conversations around school the next day and on the radio and television. I was disappointed when he lost the heavyweight championship to Leon Spinks and elated when Ali defeated Spinks in the rematch.

The first time I watched a live boxing match was when Larry Holmes defeated Ken Norton for the heavyweight belt. I recall the punches that were exchanged and the sweat that made both fighters' heads look gray. Larry Holmes was the second fighter I followed, until he lost the championship to Michael Spinks.

Pro-football was another favorite sport. I even had Pittsburgh Steelers pajamas. The earliest jerseys that I saw on television were those of the Steelers, Oakland Raiders, Chicago Bears, and the Dallas Cowboys. The 1982 NFC championship between the Cowboys and the San Francisco 49ers where Dwight Clark made the catch, and the following Super Bowl between San Francisco and the Cincinnati Bengals were both firsts for me. As I watched my television set for both of those games, it set the stage for what football is all about, as far as I was concerned.

In baseball, the first game I remember watching on television was a couple of games in the National League championship between the Philadelphia Phillies and the Houston Astros in 1980. Something about the Astros uniform and those orange white and black colors plus the star and their jersey stood out in my mind. The World Series that followed between the Phillies and the Kansas City Royals kick started my interest in Major League Baseball and winners.

NBA basketball became a part of my life thanks to CBS and the games that came on after the 10:00 p.m. news went off the air on Friday night. I watched the Lakers, Sixers, and Spurs more than any other teams for some reason, maybe because they featured players like Kareem Abdul-Jabbar, Dr. J (Julius Erving), and George "The Iceman" Gervin.

During the early 1980s, I became familiar with college basketball—teams like DePaul, Old Dominion, Loyola, Indiana, Louisville, Minnesota, and Notre Dame. When Michael Jordan hit the game-winning shot that gave North Carolina a victory over

Georgetown in the 1982 NCAA championship game, I was sitting on the floor watching the game on television with my parents. I didn't know that I was watching greatness in the making or that Jordan would turn out to be one of the greatest basketball players who ever lived.

When I take a look across the sport scene—boxing, baseball, football, and basketball—and do a "then versus now" survey. I am inclined to say the past was better.

Take boxing, for example. If someone had told me that there wouldn't be any up-and-coming tough and talented black challengers or champions in the heavyweight division in the early twenty-first century, I'd say that they were crazy. That was a tradition started by Jack Johnson and carried on by Joe Louis, Ali, Holmes, Joe Frazier, George Foreman, Mike Tyson, Evander Holyfield, and others. Echoing some whites in the past, I now am looking for the Great Black Hope to win the heavyweight championship.

I'd take a nonblack heavyweight champion, as long as he was an American, but there hasn't been a great white American heavyweight champion since Rocky Marciano in 1952, which was a long time ago. The politics involved in boxing and the sparring matches disguised as big fights because they rake in millions are becoming all too common. Whenever a pay-per-view featuring a big fight is announced, I'm stuck deciding whether to order the fight or not. I think about the last fight and how boring it was, and I'm tempted to skip the event and keep my cash. Fans that used to be upset about early-round Mike Tyson knockouts got more for their money than they get in many so-called big matches today.

The lack of top-level talent in the smaller weight classes causes over-the-hill boxers with big names to stick around far too long to keep the sport interesting. The result is boring fights and easy paydays. It's even hard to get the top fighters to fight one another at times. There is too much picking over opponents to find the least amount of resistance with biggest payday. The big fights that put great against great—such as Aaron Pryor versus Alexis Argüello In 1982 and 83, Sugar Ray Leonard versus Thomas Hearns in 1981, Julio Cesar Chavez versus Meldrick Taylor in 1990, Leonard versus Roberto Duran, two fights 1980 or Hearns versus Marvin Hagler in 1985—where are they? The three rounds that Hagler and Hearns fought in 1985 would top most of the championship matches that I see today in the middleweight and welterweight divisions.

I don't care if a fighter has millions of dollars or fancy cars. I care that he takes care of business in the ring. I don't mind bragging and trash talking; I actually love it as long as the fighter backs it up in the ring. I understand that a champion can't fight every fighter that crawls out of the woodwork. But a small circle of elite fighters needs to mix it up; they have to fight one another to determine the best of the era. How could Sugar Ray Leonard be considered one of the best if he didn't fight Hearns, Duran, or Hagler?

I long for the days of Julio Cesar Chavez, Pernell Whitaker, Mike McCallum, Donald Curry, Hector "Macho" Camacho, Michael Nunn, Iran Barkley, and Alexis Argüello. Boxers like these gentlemen were top-level talent who went at one another to determine who the best was. As far as I'm concerned, there is no pound-for-pound best boxer in this current era. That title still belongs to Sugar Ray Robinson, in my opinion.

For many fans, the Olympics is the place to see your first glimpse of the up-and-coming fighters. Unfortunately, we just don't hear about or see as many good black fighters in the Olympics lately, especially in the heavyweight class. Fighters like Sugar Ray Leonard, Muhammad Ali, George Foreman, Evander Holyfield, and others gained their fame in the Olympics before going on to become great professional fighters.

I can't believe that my first love in sports, boxing, has become a shadow of its former self. I'm a sucker though and, as a fan, I always hope that the next big fight will be a great match. The anticipation of a good fight is what keeps my attention, but I'm still waiting. And I am often disappointed. In my opinion, boxing is currently terrible; it is an almost-dead sport that needs new and talented blood to save it.

My second-favorite sport, football, is still a physical game, despite the changes to the rules about how and where to hit an opposing player, which has made the game softer. But it also has its flaws. Besides the fact that far too many players think that they are rappers and gangsters, there is far too much celebrating in the NFL for menial gains or for simply doing one's job. In particular, wide receivers have become football jesters with big mouths and not enough big catches. The rule changes that protect the quarterback also benefit wide receivers, who no longer get smacked in the mouth or a forearm to the chin during a tackle. This had led to some wide receivers to having more mouth than game.

I don't get it when a wide receiver makes a catch that a pro is supposed to make for a first down, and motions with his hands and body that it was a first down. What is that? Dude, you made one measly catch; now you think you're the next Jerry Rice. The greatest wide receiver of all time, Jerry Rice didn't have to gesture; he just busted his opponent's asses and won championships. There are exceptions. Michael Irvin was a notorious showboat, but he also happened to be one of the hardest-working players on the team, the first at practice and the last to leave. At times, he worked to exhaustion, even puking on the practice field according to stories reported on ESPN and other NFL networks Irvin was a vocal leader when his team members needed a push. He is nicknamed "the playmaker" because he made plays when it counted with his hands, not his mouth, and he won championships.

End-zone celebrations, although some have gotten out of hand with the premeditated antics, are cool as long as the team is not being blown out in the game. There are players who celebrate one catch while their team is on a drive with yards to go. What happens if the next play is a turnover? I can understand a receiver who has a tough defensive back covering him getting a little pumped up after he makes three or more consecutive catches. Football is a game of emotion, after all. I can understand and appreciate the emotion such a physical sport brings. But come on, a simple first down and not on a game-winning drive? Why are you motioning "first down" with your hands?

The players are bigger and stronger now, but I don't believe that they are necessarily more skilled than the players who came before. In fact, I would say the opposite is true. Look at the number of dropped balls by so-called professional wide receivers. Sure, today's receivers are bigger and stronger than most cornerbacks were, but many can't catch a football on a consistent basis. What they do have are big mouths, despite not winning or even competing for a damn thing. I don't care about anything players do or if they change their names. I only care that you produce on the field and try like hell to win.

I miss the old-school cornerbacks like Deion Sanders, Darrell Green, Everson Walls, Lester Hayes, Mike Haynes, and Ronnie Lott. Among today's players, Darrelle Revis is often mentioned as being a shutdown cornerback. It's possible a case could be made for a few others, but nothing that will convince me to put them in the league with past greats.

Another problem I have with the NFL is that, in my opinion, there are many mediocre teams but not enough great ones. Parity and free agency have taken their toll on the league. Hype from the media and overrated players make many teams seem better than they really are. Most NFL teams are nothing more than middle-of-the-pack average from what I see on the field.

Thankfully there are teams with a history of winning, like the Pittsburgh Steelers or the Green Bay Packers. Those teams, along with the Dallas Cowboys, New York Giants, and Chicago Bears, always generate interest and are always potential title contenders and Super Bowl winners. Now thanks to Bill Belichick and Tom Brady, we have the New England Patriots dynasty.

There are still players who try to be the best in the NFL and play at a high level. Football and other sports are supposed to be about the pursuit of and the commitment to excellence, not to mediocrity and being overpaid.

As far as I am concerned, the NBA is filled with underachieving and overpaid athletes. The mere physicality of football, in which one play might be your last and the effect the game has on the body, warrants hazard pay of some kind, along with medical coverage. The NBA, however, has so many bad teams that if some were eliminated, I would not miss them at all. Currently, there are probably six or seven elite teams in the NBA, and in my opinion a twelve-team league like existed in the 1950s and 1960s had would be sufficient today. Unofficially, The NBA is a twelve-team league already, with all the average players on bad teams that play basketball the wrong way in my opinion.

The NBA must be rewarding the newer generation of players for the contributions of previous players; that's the only thing that explains why the NBA is as popular around the world as it is today. It surely can't be because current players deserve it. Too many players in the NBA don't work hard enough, on and off the court, to be considered great or even good by true sport fans who look past the glamour and the lights.

Why hasn't anyone since Dennis Rodman averaged eighteen rebounds a game? Rodman did it twice, in 1992 and 1993, then followed up with seventeen rebounds a game in 1994. He was a beast on the boards who hustled and played hard. Despite all the big and athletic players in the league today, no one has been able to top or match the effort of the six-foot-six Rodman.

In a league where big men shoot three pointers and long jumpers more than they post up or rebound and block shots, players doing the dirty work down low, collecting big rebounding numbers, are almost nonexistent. Big men like Moses Malone lived in the paint; they collected plenty of rebounds, both offensive and defensive. The effort seems to be lacking from many of today's players.

The retirement of Shaquille O'Neal in 2011 marked the end of an era. We will probably never see a center as big, strong, or as dominating as Shaq was. He played where big men are supposed to play—in the paint, in the middle. Dwight Howard comes close to Shaq, defensively and rebound wise. But unless he becomes a consistent offensive threat and puts up scoring averages of more than twenty-five points a game for a season or two, and does it consistently as O'Neal did, forget about it. Howard is a solid player; he has worked on his game since he entered the league, but he is no superman and shouldn't be allowed to use a title of superman until he earns it the way that Shaq did. Those who want to look at this any other way obviously don't know much about basketball or didn't see Shaq play.

The big men, those six-foot-six or taller, who refuse to rebound, have post moves, and post up on the block, are joined by three-pointer happy guards and forwards in not playing the game the way the greats did. I don't see as much dribble penetration and movements toward the basket as I used to. I remember watching Isaiah Thomas drive to the hoop and score a basket or get fouled, or do both things in many instances. Some say that Dr. J didn't shoot the ball as well as others. That's more of a compliment to his talents and his will more than anything. That meant that when he was going to the rim, the opposing team knew it and had to stop him from doing so. I remember Magic Johnson putting defenders on his hip and backing them down toward the basket to get a good shot.

In the current era, many players take the easy way out and settle for long jumpers and three pointers rather than breaking down the defense, many can't master the twenty-foot jump shot. It's either a dunk, long jumper, or three-point shot, but nothing in-between for many players in the NBA. Many of today's players do not work hard enough, in my opinion, on or off the court. Kobe Bryant works to improve his game during the off season. It's in the off-season that average players become good players, and good players become great ones. Many of the so-called stars just don't get it. Bryant is a student of the game, the best since Jordan; he has wanted to be great since he entered the league, perhaps earlier. He is the Michael Jordan of the current NBA, but he is second to Jordan in terms of the game overall.

Jordan had grit; Jordan was tenacious; Jordan never settled on the court. A tough defense and age may have forced him to shoot jumpers, but he tried to get as close to the hoop as possible to make his shots. He exploded into the NBA, averaging twenty-eight points a game as a rookie. Many of his points were from layups and dunks, as he took entire teams to the basket. Jordan mastered the twenty-foot jump shot and made three pointers when he had to. He was unstoppable.

I've watched several NBA games in which professional athletes go up and down the floor, take bad shot after bad shot, and miss shot after shot off the rim. Some refuse to adjust their game to the moment and just keep shooting the threes and the long jumpers. If Jordan missed a couple of jumpers, he would post up on the block and try for an easier shot or to get fouled.

Jordan made an impact on the game on either side of the ball. He was a notorious shutdown defender as his ten all-defensive first-team selections show. He did whatever it took to win. Even before the Chicago Bulls became champions, when they were losing to the Detroit Pistons and the Boston Celtics, Jordan went down with both guns blazing. He tried hard, getting to game seven of the Eastern Conference finals in 1990 against Detroit before losing the series 4 to 3. To win, Mike had to learn to trust his teammates, and Scottie Pippen, John Paxson, Horace Grant, and the others had to step up their games in order for the Bulls to eventually win a championship.

Team ball and playing the right way is even more important now in the NBA, with the implementing of the zone, which makes the pro game look like a high-school or college game. Man-to-man, "stop me if you can," or double—and triple-team defense are what I thought the NBA was all about. But now the game is apparently about making things easier for players who can't defend. This and other factors, like overpaying athletes, have made the NBA soft. The physical games that were played involved trash talking, pushing and shoving, and sometimes fighting, made for great games. It also made for great TV, endless rivalries, and good basketball being played the right way.

The Celtics versus the Lakers in the 1980s, the Celtics versus the Sixers in the early 1980s, the Pistons versus the Bulls in the late 1980s and early 1990s, the Bulls versus the New York Knicks in the 1990s—those rivalries had everything a fan could want and more: good basketball and players who hated each other on the court and would give their all, even blood, for their teams in hopes of winning a championship.

The NBA may be a soft and dressed-up high-school game, but Major League Baseball (MLB) is still close to what it once was. Baseball is a highly skilled sport; if players do not compete and get the job done, they may be demoted to the minors. Baseball is a highly competitive sport; hitting the fastball or curveball, throwing strikes and great fielding make this game special and are the reason why it will always be America's favorite past time.

The only changes in baseball today are the treatment of pitchers. The number of innings pitched is more closely monitored, and fewer complete games are pitched. Another change is the low number of black players who are currently in Major League Baseball. In 1986 according to USA today 28 percent of Major League Baseball players were black. The latest polls show that number at 8 percent.

Why are pitchers pulled from games so early? At this rate, who will be the next three-hundred-game winner in baseball? Are the pitchers of today in not as strong as pitchers who came before them? Do they tire more easily?

Latino players and players from the Caribbean are replacing American blacks, who seem to have lost interest in the sport in high numbers. USA today polls also show that there is a 68 percent population of blacks in the NFL and that the NBA has a 82 percent black ratio. Football and Basketball seem to be more appealing to young black males today. Part of the reason for this as it relates to today is the NBA and NFL has been affected by hip-hop culture. Baseball doesn't have the street appeal that it once had. You don't hear about baseball players popping bottles of champagne or making it rain like you hear about some football and basketball players. You even hear professional athletes like boxers enter rings to rap songs, NBA hoopsters and NFL players rap along to a popular rap song or even make a rap album themselves.

Baseball will survive, despite the lack of interest on the part of many young blacks, just as it did before blacks were allowed to play. But, damn, it would be good to have more Hank Aarons, Willie Mays, Reggie Jackson's, Frank Robinsons, Eddie Murray's, Bob Gibson's, Dave Winfield's, Kirby Puckett's, and Willie Stargells.

I do have a problem with Barry Bonds being vilified more than others over the steroid issue. Bonds, Mark McGwire, Sammy Sosa, Raphael Palmero, David Ortiz, Manny Ramirez, and Roger Clemens were all accused of taking steroids. But except for

Bonds, the white sports writers don't roast and spit venom on these players. In my opinion, Barry Bonds is not liked because he didn't kiss ass during his playing days the way that Sosa did. He wasn't an all-American white boy like McGwire was. So what if Bonds didn't like the judgmental media? They weren't his friends. I read what they say about Bonds, and none of it was friendly. Why does he have to act a certain way and be a good boy? Since his playing days are done, and there is some dirt on him, the vultures are circling him as if they have been waiting a long time for his downfall. Now many have their chance to judge him even more. But no one can take away his pretty swing, his MVPs, or his 762 home runs.

The writers and the media remind me of the Chicago Cubs, who only want Jell-O pudding, nonthreatening black players. That's why they haven't won a World Series in more than one hundred years. Players like Lou Brock, Bill Madlock and Joe Carter should be thankful that they got away from such a franchise and were able to win championships. In my opinion, the Cubs are so accustomed to making all the wrong moves that when they do sign a brother they sign one like Milton Bradley in 2009. The only problem was Bradley had too much attitude and not enough talent. After the team tanked in yet another season, Bradley was named as the scapegoat. What about the other one hundred years? Whose fault was that?

There is no curse; it's all in the way the Cubs do business. The Cubs are the only team that did not display Jackie Robinson's retired jersey number. Dusty Baker recalled that during his final months as team manager someone took a bowel movement in the spot where he stood in the dugout. My older family members have always told me that the Cubs was a racist organization that played in a racist neighborhood. When I was a kid, my dad and uncle were attacked by white males as we were driving away from Wrigley Field after a Cubs game.

Baseball and boxing are similar in that they require high skill and discipline to be one of the best. In boxing you have to train hard to be the best. Running, dieting, lifestyle, and skill play a major role in determining a boxer's success. There is a new generation of brothers who don't want to work too hard. They want it easy; they don't want to train, they want to make it rain.

Behind the glamour lies a painful reality that showed itself during the 2011 NBA lockout, when players and owners went back and forth over income. The owners wanted a bigger share of players' income off the court, their endorsements, etc. The players balked initially and threatened to sit out an entire season. It was tough talk, but the reality was that many of the players simply couldn't afford to sit out an entire season. They have been too busy making it rain and haven't put enough away for a rainy day. If the players were going to fold, which is what they did, they should have folded in the summer, started the season on time and not wasted the fan's time with nonsense.

I have always believed that NBA led by David Stern was a racist league, just not openly racist. The zone, the dress code for players, issuing technical fouls to players for talking or complaining to referees are just the latest assaults on black players. I thought this would have been the perfect time for black players, entertainers, and businessmen to form an independent league similar to the American Basketball Association (ABA) I should have known better because that's not how most black people think.

Today, sports are heavily influenced by street and hip-hop culture. Many young athletes, especially black ones, are caught up in this culture and can't escape the situations that sometimes arise from street influence. In cities across this country, where blacks and poverty run rampant, there are drug dealers, pimps, gangbangers, thieves, and murderers. Many black professional athletes come from these neighborhoods. In many cases their friends and associates partake in these activities.

Champagne sipping and *MTV Cribs*—"look at my big house, you poor fool; look at how many Bentleys I have and look at my rims"—have made money an even greater root of evil in the ghetto. The combination of the "money right now" era with jealousy of those who don't have as much or aren't as popular as others leads to athletes being involved in fights and shootings in clubs. In the hood, often the drug dealers and punks are the ones in the clubs drinking good champagne, spending cash, and meeting women. They are the ones being treated like stars by other patrons and employees. Many admire them because they're "ballers," as they say. When the black athletes go to the clubs, the drug dealer isn't treated like a star anymore. Now, there's an NBA or NFL player in the house. The women who thought the dealer was hot last night now watch the athletes' pop bottles and spend cash. The club employees explain that the drug dealer can't enter the VIP area, perhaps not even the club at all. He becomes jealous and enraged and may pick a fight, or worse, with an athlete.

We hear the terms "keeping it real" and "staying true to your roots" all the time. Being true means understanding who your people are and how they behave at times. This means you have to stay away from the clowns, pick better places to hang out, or stay home in order to enjoy what you have worked hard for.

Black athletes should know that jealously runs rampant in the black community. Many black people are crabs in the barrel, who crawl on top of one another to get out and work to keep others from succeeding. Sometimes in order to enjoy your success, you have to surround yourself with successful people. When successful brothers are in the same club with street brothers, there's bound to be some jealousy. I'm not rich or famous, and there are some people that I would never want to associate with. Unequally yoked people can't exist in the same area without some conflict of morals and values.

Associating with the friends you grew up with is okay if they are the right type of friends. Friends who use you for your money and fame, those who are jealous of but need what you have aren't friends; they're leeches and dangerous to both your bank account and your life. If one is lucky enough to have one friend or relative who will assess you and your situation honestly, then that is an advantage. I am not talking about groupies who will tell you how great you are and kiss your ass because you are feeding them. I am talking about someone—a mother, father, brother, sister, someone close who you can trust to help keep you grounded, someone who is appreciative of all that you have. A strong base will tell you that you need to work on your game or which situations to avoid.

In previous years, gambling, and alcohol and drug addictions were the issues that troubled certain players. Now there are those same vices, plus fights, shootings, stabbings, murders, and arrests. A lot of this stems from street culture, the focus of money, and the "all eyes on me" behavior, which is considered to be the cure to all that ails people. With so much focus on glamour and money, the black race must be the wealthiest group in America. It's the most insane thing to me, that the poorest and most dependent race of people on the planet talk the most shit about money,

Athletes make more money now than they did before. Million-dollar contracts and bonuses are common in certain sports now, even the NFL, which for years lagged behind basketball and baseball in terms of wages. The street culture is a big part of many young athletes' lives; when that is combined with big money, some athletes go overboard and even think they are untouchable. Some think they can do whatever they want, even sell drugs and murder.

"Pacman" Jones made it rain in Las Vegas in 2007, throwing money in the air because that's what the rappers sang about. If players didn't make as much money or if their salaries were tied to performance, you'd see a change in their behavior. The true knuckleheads, of course, will continue to be so until they are kicked out of the league and end their careers. I don't have a problem with players being paid large sums of money, as long as they earn it and make a contribution to the league with their skills.

I do have a problem with players entering the league before they are ready. In the NBA, this has become a norm and is one of the reasons for the bad basketball that I often see. In fact, in the last several years, I have waited until the playoffs start, when the worst teams are out and the bad ones will soon be eliminated, before I watch NBA games. Kobe Bryant and Kevin Garnett went to the NBA straight after high school, avoiding college, kick-starting a trend among many young athletes, especially black basketball players. Both Bryant and Garnett had talent, but they had to work their tails off in order for that talent to bloom in the NBA. Previously, Moses Malone and Darryl Dawkins were the most notable players to jump to the NBA from high school. Dawkins broke backboards, nicknamed his dunks, and played alongside Dr. J in Philadelphia early in his career before finishing his career overseas, becoming a fan favorite. Malone went on to become one of the greatest centers ever by working up a sweat and becoming a scoring and rebounding machine.

The NBA requiring one year of college before turning pro is a great rule, but requiring players to wait two years would be better. Players attempting to duplicate Bryant and Garnett end up sitting on the bench or put up small numbers in points, rebounds, assists, or steals. They would be better off in college, where they could develop their game and contribute to a college basketball team by winning games and titles.

A boy who is not prepared to play with men or is unwilling to put in the work that is required for success hurts the league. Today's league is more about tattoos and braids—which I despise because they don't belong on a basketball court; what league is this, the NBA or the WNBA? There is not enough focus on the game of basketball itself. There is a lot of expression on the court, but not enough of it is on what it takes to win and be the best. Simply put, many of today's NBA players aren't that good.

With all the sideshows going on, the NBA has turned to foreign players to keep white spectators in the stands. Many white fans have grown tired of the antics of some black players. I often tell my friends that white people aren't going to keep paying big bucks to watch clowns run up and down the court, throwing up goofy hand symbols when they hit a three-point shot.

You know something is wrong when the NBA has to tell grown men how to dress when they enter an arena. I can't believe that millionaires will not wear suits or nice slacks and a shirt or a sport coat unless they are directed to do so. Patrick Ewing, Julius Erving, Michael Jordan, Dominique Wilkins, and Hakeem Olajuwon were sharply dressed. Watching players dressed that sharp was like watching *GQ* magazine in the flesh.

It's important for the black players, especially now, to set the example of how to look when you are entering a place of business. Some say the way you're dressed shouldn't matter. For a young person to see one of his favorite players dressed for success is inspiring; the young person needs to see someone who looks like him dressing as a man should rather than wearing basketball jerseys, blue jeans, and gym shoes to appeal to the street mentality. That attitude is encouraging young black men to die in the streets and fill up the prisons.

I know that many athletes feel that they are not role models. I totally agree with them, because no one is perfect; we all make mistakes. A bad decision by an idolized sports figure often turns that person into a villain. In addition, some athletes embrace the same culture that is destroying many young blacks. Personally, I feel that an athlete who embraces the negative aspects of black culture is more of a detriment than a role model to young black people.

The answers to some of the problems are the ones we often hear. More black men need to raise their children so that not having a father is no longer a reason for the recklessness of some athletes. Young players also should take money-management classes to avoid excessive spending and ending up broke. It would be great if more athletes stayed in school long enough to develop both physically and mentally. How about learning some post moves if you're a big man, or tightening up on your defense, learning how to box out, and becoming a better rebounder? I'm tired of seeing players turn pro before they're ready to contribute to the game simply because they can't wait for the riches that will come. Every man would buy his mother a house if he could, and if you're good enough to turn pro, you will be able to do so. I know that many are poor and need the money immediately, but doesn't the integrity of the game matter? Who is in it for the money, and who is in it for the love of the game?

When I speak about love of the game, I speak about Bryant, Garnett, Ray Allen, Tim Duncan, Dirk Nowitzki, Dwyane Wade, Derrick Rose, Jason Kidd, Tony Parker, and LeBron James, and a few others. Then there are those who should have stayed in school and learned the game of basketball instead of diminishing the skill level and the legacy of the NBA. We are witnessing a total disrespect to the contributions and accomplishments by some of the greatest players in NBA history right before our eyes.

The pressures to leave school early to make millions are even greater now with the exploitation or pimping of college athletes by the schools and the National Collegiate Atheletics Association (NCAA). Basketball and football players generate millions of dollars for many schools. Bowl games and March Madness give the players exposure, while everyone involved get paid. It doesn't matter if the players go pro or not; the schools still profit.

It's easy for me to suggest that players should stay in school more than one year, when I'm not the one being pimped by the NCAA.

Many college athletes are treated like pros; they travel like pros, are admired, and sign autographs. Yet when it comes to getting paid, they are treated like amateurs and punished for taking a dime or a sandwich from a booster

Players are aware of the dollars that are generated off their backs, particularly since many of them come from families with little or no money. How can the NCAA or anyone not understand that players will be tempted by cash and gifts? To punish those who do accept cash or other perks is insane as is making coaches out to be bad guys and firing them because they know that the kids are being pimped. They know how hard their players work and how broke some of them are. What is a coach supposed to do, report this poor kid, whose scholarship represented the only way to go to school? If this current pattern continues, then I completely understand why a talented player would leave school early and take his shot at the pros rather than continue to be pimped by the NCAA.

Why not eliminate this system altogether? Why not award the players who generate millions of dollars a monthly portion? The schools that football or basketball programs generate the most money would of course pay more to the players. Until this happens there will always be some story about a player profiting from his exposure. If that doesn't happen then, the exploitation and the punishment will continue. To the black athletes who have been are affected by this exploitation or have been punished for accepting gifts, it would have been nice to see your talents at an HBCU (historically black college and university) where your talents are greatly needed.

HBCUs were created in an era when black and white people couldn't attend the same schools. Cheyney University, founded in Pennsylvania in 1837, was the first institution to advocate that black people should be able to get a higher education. Why did blacks turn away from this? The tools for blacks to succeed and earn respect in this country, rather than begging for acceptance have been put in place, but have not been fully taken advantage by.

Many of the biggest stars and record holders in the NFL attended HBCUs: Walter Payton, Jerry Rice, Willie Lanier, Mel Blount, and Everson Walls are a few examples. In the NBA, Willis Reed and Avery Johnson attended black colleges. Schools like Grambling, Alcorn, Jackson State, Howard, and Morgan State were established for black people to excel in academics, student government and athletics.

Talk about forgetting where you come from. As soon as Master, I mean, as soon as white colleges and universities opened their doors to blacks, all was forgotten, and the flood gates opened. Schools like the University of Kentucky that once refused to have black players on their basketball team became teams of smiling jacks saying, "Yes sir boss." The pattern of blacks following whites proves that many blacks do feel that they are inferior to whites when it comes to education and athletics. Now we know that many thoughts about white superiority come from black people themselves.

Now, of course, one can attend any school that one chooses. I didn't attend an HBCU, which remains my biggest regret, but the facts are the facts. The interest in and funding of black colleges has declined, but thank God many still do attend HBCUs. Imagine if talented black athletes had gone to black colleges. The effect that would have had on black colleges would have been staggering. No black college has won a Division I NCAA championship, college World Series, or an NCAA bowl game. Is this a coincidence or is this somehow due to the behavior of black people? How can you win when your best talent is being recruited by nonblack colleges and universities? Some may feel that the black colleges don't offer the same type of exposure that white dominated Universities can. Bull, let me tell you something. First, good is good; it is practically guaranteed that if you're good enough, you will get your shot. Those who aren't good enough won't go pro, no matter what school they go to. Play the game well enough, and you will get the exposure and results that you are looking for. Besides most student athletes don't go pro anyway; most have careers in other areas.

If the Fabulous Five had displayed their talents at a HBCU instead of Michigan, their influence would have been unprecedented, and many would have followed. Chris Webber, Jalen Rose, Jimmy King, Juwan Howard, and Ray Jackson could have been the catalysts for a bigger movement, instead of seasons being erased from the books and back to back appearances in the NCAA final four in 1992 and 1993 banners taken down. The NCAA and the HBCUs would have their best athletes competing against one another, creating classic moments for all sports fans to enjoy, making the sport better for everyone involved. College sports would be bigger and better than it is now.

This isn't about separation; it's about education, because black colleges still exist in America. No one complains about white-dominated universities; they're accepted as the norm. What's wrong with black colleges being promoted and raised to a more respectful and lucrative status? There are options and hope. If it's not too late, try a HBCU. They desperately need black students and athletes. How much of an effect on young black athletes would a Bowl Championship Series (BCS) title win by Grambling have? How historic would it be to see an HBCU team cut down the net during March Madness? Of course, it is important for black colleges to continue to ensure that students get an education; those who want to learn must be taught.

Something I never understood about the civil rights movement was its attitude toward education. I never understood why black people insisted on being educated at white schools. What was wrong with black people being educated by black people? Surely there were black teachers available for black children. Rights were granted during the civil rights movement; why weren't funds allotted to black schools and children? In 1957, the Little Rock Nine, those nine black students who were escorted by the National Guard to desegregate Central High School, may represent a historic moment to most people. But to me, that event furthers the belief that white people are smarter than black people and are better teachers. Or was this just another case of black people wanting to go to the school that was barred to them by law?

White people weren't protesting to go to school with black people; most felt more comfortable being among their own. Yet some make that sound like a sin. I don't see it that way at all. Why couldn't more blacks do the same? Why must some continue to look to master for instruction? Does that picture of white Jesus in black churches make people believe that the white man is God and has all the answers to our problems?

If black people are to have a prominent place in society, there has to be an increase in black male teacher educating young black males in grade and high school. Unless black men teach and provide life experiences to young black males, many who come from broken homes, the black race will stay behind. The only thing in which black males lead other races is the rate of incarceration and early deaths.

Black people can't complain about biased exams or that their real history and contributions to American society have been left out of the history books. This is the system that you wanted to belong to, right? So shut up, quit your whining, and enjoy your view.

I've heard the argument that going to a black college will not prepare a young black person for the real world. First of all, the saying should be, the world had better be prepared for us. Second, what are the whites who attend white schools being prepared for? Being the boss?

CHAPTER 9

PEOPLE

People make the world go round, and it takes all types to make it a world. I marvel at the patterns and behaviors of people. It seems that those who are privileged let things go to their heads a bit.

When something tragic happens in a community, a murder, for example, I hear people say, "I can't believe this has happened in this neighborhood," or "Things like that don't happen around here." Well, it did just happen; who do these people think they are? Where do these people think that they live, on the moon?

Then there are those who walk the streets freely at 3 a.m., but are shocked when they are attacked or harmed in some way. I don't know if it's a lack of common sense or street sense, a sense of privilege, or a combination of all three, but I was always told to watch my back when I was out, especially at night. It doesn't matter that you live in an upscale community. Thieves, rapists, and others are everywhere. Often, the brave ones travel to communities outside their own, especially upscale areas because that's where residents don't expect crime to happen.

Everyone has heard stories about nonblack convenient store owners and employees excessively watching the black patrons, who are quickly approached with a "may I help you?" The way a person is dressed will not make any difference. Take the hoodie, for example; white people wear them just as much as black people do, but in my experience, few if any eyebrows are raised when they do. White America doesn't feel threatened by white people wearing hoodies.

When some people in white communities discuss a suspect charged with a crime like rape or murder, they are shocked to find that the suspect is the nice or quiet neighbor who minded his own business. For the most part, white people seem to get the benefit of the doubt when it comes to crime. What else can explain how convicted murderer John Wayne Gacy was able to bury the bodies of the young males he raped and killed in his home and get away with it for so long?

I guess that being in the majority, when the greatest accomplishments made by man have been credited to your race, brings a sense of pride and a feeling of being the best. That is further validated by other races following you wherever you move, begging for your acknowledgment, hoping you'll see them as an equal. All these things could cause a sense of being better or more privileged to some degree.

However, God and nature makes no such distinctions between people. God judges all people of all races; no one is exempt from his blessings or his wrath. Hurricanes and floods that rip apart the South and run up the East Coast and tornados that sweep across the nation, ripping apart states like Texas, North Carolina, Missouri convince me that someone has his eye on America, which has to answer for its sins, past and present. I have always believed that hurricanes follow the routes that the slave ships took from Africa to America.

Speaking of the wrath of God, why is it why is it only white dudes who predict the world is going to end? Would such an important message be revealed only to a white guy? I remember the evangelist Billy Graham making a comment in a story in the news after the 7.0-magnitude earthquake that struck Haiti; he said that God was punishing Haiti for resisting and overthrowing slavery. I immediately stated that maybe God was punishing Haiti because it became such a corrupt country after such a historic triumph to free itself from bondage.

From the church, let's move to the state. A question that I repeatedly ask about the political party system is how did black people become slaves to the Democratic Party? Wasn't this the party of southern slave owners? Who would let something like this happen? In most other races, there is more of a balance between those who are Republicans and those who are Democrats. According to the PEW research center 26 percent of whites in America are Democrat, Latinos 32 percent are Democrat. Black people, are the only group in this country who overwhelmingly pledge their allegiance to one side, a whopping 69 percent of blacks are Democrats.

In Chicago, the black pastors in the big churches welcome white Democrats who are running for a major election. The pastor, the gatekeeper, gives the platform to the candidate, essentially telling the congregation which Democrat they should vote for. In effect, these pastors are helping to keep blacks enslaved to the Democratic Party and the direction that it wants to go.

Most blacks are taught to believe that the Republican Party is only for rich white people and doesn't give a damn about black people. I don't know if you can tie a belief like that to an entire party, any more than you can say that deeds done by certain Democrats mean the entire Democratic Party gives a damn about black people. If that's the case, Abraham Lincoln and Dwight Eisenhower, both Republicans, should have convinced more black people to join their party, because Lincoln freed the slaves and Eisenhower dealt with civil rights issues, like dispatching the National Guard protect the Little Rock Nine in 1957.

I have associated with white Republicans and Democrats, and I can't tell you that the Democrats treated me any better or worse than the Republicans did. Party affiliation had nothing to do with how we related to one another. Do black people believe that only Republicans call black people "niggers" and that Democrats don't?

What a luxury it must be for the Democratic Party to know that through rain, sleet, and snow, no matter how bad the economic situation, no matter how much is lacking in people's lives, it can count on the black vote on election day.

For example, former President Bill Clinton signed the NAFTA trade agreement, which has taken jobs away from the United States and sent them to other countries, leaving America with a gaping hole in manufacturing and industry, an area in which we once ruled. He also signed welfare reform legislation, which hurt many who had become too dependent on the system, causing an increase in poverty and crime in already poor black areas. He didn't make it more affordable for black people to go to college; he didn't give free college education to black people on welfare. What did he do to help black people? If you listen to black people, however, you hear that he was the first black president. Why? Because he plays the saxophone, eats chicken, and smoked weed? Maybe Clinton would be a fun guy to hang out with, but I could say the same thing for George W. Bush, who partied, drank alcohol, and did cocaine in his youth.

Many black people complained about George W. Bush. People chided Bush, calling him everything from not smart to a racist, despite the fact that he hired more blacks in his administration than President Obama did. Bush even went into the booth during a baseball game and asked Hall of Fame star Joe Morgan why more blacks weren't playing baseball, although it was better paid than other sports and resulted in longer careers. President Bush also did more to prevent the spread of diseases particualry AIDS in Africa. But Bill Clinton likes black people, and George W. Bush doesn't?

Both Republicans and Democrats look after the interest of banks, the automobile industry, oil companies, big business, and special interest groups. Gas and light companies, the media, and other large corporations enjoy perks from both sides of the aisle. I can't honestly say that one group or another looks out for the interest of the American people. It's childish and naïve for black people to believe that only the Republicans look out for the interest of these groups. Both sides of the aisle are responsible for the mess in this country. The rich still get richer, and the poor get poorer. But there are still those who believe that party affiliation has something to do with it.

Let's assume that the Republican Party is only for the rich, as many say. Why shouldn't prosperity be a goal of one of the poorest of races in America? What's wrong with improving one's economic and social conditions? Some would rather listen to the excuses that many Democrats and others offer as the reasons why many black people lag behind everyone else. Black people are the biggest consumers in America; many spend money and live beyond their means like they are the rich people that the Republicans supposedly represent. So I guess when things don't go their way and they are broke, some blame the Republicans. But when they are in the stores buying Coogi and other expensive clothing, everything is fine.

While many are suffering, the special-interest groups are gaining more power. PETA (People of the Ethical Treatment of Animals) is an example of a special-interest group that has been given power by the government to control the lives of others. I know that animals, especially dogs and cats, have special places in the lives of many. I am not downplaying the love that many have for their pets. But some people receive no jail time for harming human beings. Black people have been murdered at the hands of whites who have not spent one day in jail for the act. "You can kill a black person, but don't let me see you hurting a dog" is the saying I use. PETA, the media, and the white masses make sure

117

that those who abuse an animal are met with justice, but they turn a blind eye to police brutality and the mistreatment of others. Where are the protests when injustices are done to humans?

If you're black, dog fighting is yet another excuse to lock you up in prison, give you a criminal record, and complicate or destroy your life. I read an article online that PETA now wants to launch a pornography site to promote its campaign against animal abuse. What a moral group they are, upholding the values of American society.

I know that there are those who are privileged, elitist, and suppressive, who like to control everything, but real life doesn't always work out that way. Take, for instance, certain drugs like crack cocaine and heroin, which were confined to black areas. No one could predict that white adults and teens from the suburbs would drive to the city in such volume to get these drugs. Life isn't Hollywood, it isn't scripted, and you can't control the outcome.

There are enough scripts in Hollywood as it is, where corny movies, with corny actors and actresses, are shown as stars and as glamorous. Once a year, one of those corny movies wins an Oscar and an over glorified actor and actress win an Academy Award. I don't think I have ever watched an Academy Award presentation in my life. The movies or actors or directors that I think should win don't and, more important, black movies, actors, and directors don't win enough. I am a black man in America; why shouldn't I want to see a reflection of my likeness winning awards like everyone else? Ten or eleven winners in more than eighty years of Oscar ceremonies don't give me much reason to ever watch an Academy Award presentation.

I guess it doesn't bother black people in Hollywood because, year after year, they sit and hope that this is the year that the black quota will be filled. I don't know why blacks don't create an equal counterpart to the Oscars and skip the Oscars. What message have we been sending to the younger generation—that even though some have "arrived" and are successful, we still need approval and validation from the white establishment to show we're good enough?

When Jesse Jackson called for black people to boycott the Oscars, I thought it was one of his best ideas. A permanent boycott of the Oscars along with an equivalent ceremony for black actors, actresses, directors, etc., could set the stage for another Black Renaissance. The problem is not enough black people supported Jackson. If they had, our future in movies at all levels would be that much brighter. But black actors in Hollywood obviously don't want this to happen for the usual reasons—dependency, fear, and greed. Until then, movies awarded based on politics and who's prominent. And if the past holds true, the award winners almost always will be nonblack.

It actually makes sense that black people don't receive as many Academy Awards as white people do. I don't believe the Academy Awards were invented with black people in mind; they were invented to award the white people with accolades and praise. I don't have a problem with that at all; I just wish that the black filmmakers in Hollywood would do something about it instead of selling out as usual. Times have changed; this isn't the golden era of Hollywood. The so-called stars of today have nothing on the ones of yesteryear. The days with leading men like Humphrey Bogart, Clark Gable, Gary Cooper, and Burt Lancaster and others are long gone. Most of the leading men today are nothing more than punks compared to men like them.

Liz Taylor's passing marked the end of an era for glamorous women in Hollywood, in my opinion. Marilyn Monroe, Audrey Hepburn, Ginger Rogers, Ava Gardner, Mae West, Jane Russell, and Taylor were glamorous. Taylor stayed sharp in her attire, the diamonds she wore, in almost all of her public appearances until she wasn't healthy. Now, bony, anorexic women are paraded on my television set or on a movie screen, and I'm told that they are glamorous. Yeah, right.

In today's Hollywood, the lights still shine bright. But when I mentioned to my daughter that Hollywood was where many movie stars lived, she shrugged her shoulders and said, "So what? Hollywood is ghetto." That's the perfect word to summarize today's Hollywood, an over dramatized and phony ghetto. And I'm not interested.

CHAPTER 10

WHAT NOW?

The 1712 Willie Lynch letter which I happened to read in a library instructed white Virginians how to keep their slaves under control is still an effective tool for controlling the lives and destinies of a high percentage of blacks in America. Who would have thought a letter could control the course of an entire race for three hundred years?

The first part of the letter instructs white people to keep black people totally dependent on them for survival. We know this is still true about everything from education, food, and clinics to the building of homes, commercial properties, and jobs. The fact is, the black race is almost totally dependent on the white race for its survival.

The letter also talks about pitting black males against black females. God knows, this indeed is a fact; black men and women are constantly at odds over children, money, roles, and power. Black men father children and disappear, causing resentment among the mothers who are left to raise the children alone. Black women are so angry in many cases that child-support money becomes their only concern, not the time that the father could spend with the child. The black community is filled with furious mothers and absent fathers, with the consequences being more division among an already divided group.

Now more than ever, black women are the sole providers for their families. Some of these women have professional jobs and earn big paychecks. You hear about black professional women who complain of how it's hard to find a black man of an equal status. The women who feel this way say there aren't enough professional black men in corporate America; therefore they have no one of color to date. That's an insult to men who aren't professional but work hard and earn decent paychecks. Just because a black man doesn't wear a suit and make $80,000 a year, does that mean he's not compatible with a professional black woman? It seems that white corporate America is the standard for professional black women. Willie Lynch . . .

How bad is it between black males and females? A Stanford University professor named Ralph Richard Banks wrote in his book, *Is Marriage for White People: How the African American Marriage Decline Affects Everyone* (2011), that professional black women should marry out and not down. He suggests that professional black women should date white males and leave blue-collar black men behind. You hear that, black man? According to Banks, professional black women should not marry black construction workers, truck drivers, mechanics, electricians, plumbers, or railroad or crane operators. You're not man enough for a black woman, but other races are.

Meanwhile, weak black men who are unable to hear no or to control their emotions continue to stalk, physically harm, and even kill women who want to end a relationship. Hey, you weak fools, there are more women out there. What are the odds, eight females to one male? If a woman doesn't want to date you for whatever reason, who cares? Take your lumps, listen to some love songs, cry your tears, shiver in your bed, and get on with your life. There is no need for the crazy "if I can't have her, no one can" insanity.

The Willie Lynch letter also speaks about light-skinned blacks versus dark-skinned blacks. This is the most ignorant and depressing part of the entire letter; people of the same race talking in terms of a skin color is as low as you can go. I don't even know what to say about this one; it's so disturbing. That black people themselves assert that "light-skinned blacks are this" and "dark-skinned blacks are that" is amazing to me. Anyone who engages in this behavior is truly still a slave. In Africa, there are light-skinned blacks and there are dark-skinned blacks; there always have been and always will be. There is more than just one shade of black. Anyone who looks at this any other way is ignorant or stupid.

One of the last things that the letter discusses is pitting older black people against younger ones. Older people don't understand the behavior of many in the younger generation—their goofy music, disrespect, dress, or the way they loiter and litter around homes, stores, and businesses in high numbers. Many elders are afraid to walk the streets for fear of being harmed, and rightfully so. They are frequent targets of people who will rob, hurt, or kill them. They are saddened and heavily disturbed by the behavior and tactics of young black America.

The black race's future in America was predestined by white people in 1712. And many blacks have been following the manual that is the Willie Lynch letter to a T. It's almost enough to make you say, why bother? The situation for black Americans seems to be hopeless. I have to ask, if the southern states had agreed with Abraham Lincoln and the Union in 1861 and had not expanded slavery in states where it did not already exist, how many blacks would still be slaves? How many blacks would be free, and how many blacks would own slaves themselves?

Faith, and the belief that God won't allow the sufferings of blacks to be in vain, is all you can cling too. Because it seems that man has failed us, the iceberg has been hit, and the boat is sinking, slowly but surely. Who else but God can right this ship?

Muslims have Mosques to pray and Jewish people have synagogues to do so as well, but what do the black masses have? I contend that the black church was set up in the likeness of the slave masters in the South instead of reflection of our original roots. Men with flaws are leading the flawed masses, instead of imperfect individuals seeking knowledge, guidance, and forgiveness from the most high for themselves. Your preacher can't save you from the wrath of God and he does not have anything to do with the blessings you receive from God either.

In many black communities, a pastor or preacher is the most powerful and prosperous person. Religious leaders have become the spokesmen for the black agenda in many cases. Despite the chaos that exists in the black community, despite the lack of industry and business opportunities, despite the poverty and the crime, churches still are being built, and the preachers are still getting paid. The other black people and their families, children, and grandchildren will get their riches after they die, in the afterlife, right?

Millions of black slaves were shipped from Africa. The money made from slave trading and slave labor totals millions and billions of dollars. The cost of determining a race's future by white and black people alike is priceless.

The behavior of black people is so disturbing that in the forty years since his death, black people still haven't come up with a replacement for Martin Luther King Jr. His is the only name that comes up in discussions about black leaders or icons. Many black people have been trained by blacks and whites alike not to support the Nation of Islam or its leader Louis Farrakhan, despite the fact no group, social center, or black church has turned more black individuals into disciplined and productive men. The only time that the black church did something that truly benefited the black race was during the 1950s and 1960s, when Dr. King and the Southern Christian leadership Council led the civil rights movement, when they took the word of God to the street and fought for equality.

Muslim men and women are taught to live clean lifestyles—no pork, no alcohol, no revealing clothes for the women. Muslims have instilled more discipline and helped more black individuals to lead a more positive and healthy life than any black church has. And maybe that's the problem; perhaps far too many rules make a religion seem more like a cult than a way of life. I am not a Muslim. I was raised a Baptist. But the truth is the truth. Most black people will not even mention or honor Elijah Muhammad during Black History Month, despite the fact that he spoke about black people fending for themselves and building their own communities.

It's a wrap; in other words, it's over for black people in many areas. The New World looks as if Gays, Latinos and those of a mixed race; (half black and half week) are the new Negroes of America. Only God can save us from ourselves and others. Black people are doing their part to ensure that the good guys wear white and the bad guys wear black, that a black cat is bad luck, that black jellybeans taste worse than white jellybeans, or that Black Friday is used as a term for failure in the stock market. What happened to black pride, the black butterfly, and on the black side? Some are more concerned and preoccupied with being recognized as African American, when it's clear that the family structure and the community were better off when we were considered black or colored. Bourgeois Negro's? Are black Americans imitating the French now too?

Remember to remember, or we are doomed to repeat history.

REFERENCES

1. Robert Longley, "Salaries and Benefits of US Congress Members," About.com; http://usgovinfo.about.com/od/uscongress/a/congresspay.htm; accessed August 2, 2012.

2. Tracy Jan, "Harvard professor Gates arrested at Cambridge home," *Boston Globe*, July 20, 2009; http://www.boston.com/news/local/breaking_news/2009/07/harvard.html, accessed August 12, 2012.

3. See "Taser: An officer's weapon of choice," *60 Minutes*, http://www.cbsnews.com/8301-18560_162-57323531/taser-an-officers-weapon-of-choice; accessed August 12, 2012.

www.ingramcontent.com/pod-product-compliance
Lightning Source LLC
Chambersburg PA
CBHW051423280526
45785CB00003B/1135